C000257241

After Brexit, What Ne:

To Rosie

After Brexit, What Next?

Trade, Regulation and Economic Growth

Patrick Minford

Professor of Applied Economics, Cardiff Business School, Cardiff University, UK

with David Meenagh

Reader, Cardiff Business School, Cardiff University, UK

In Association with the Institute of Economic Affairs

 Edward **Elgar**
PUBLISHING

Cheltenham, UK • Northampton, MA, USA

© Patrick Minford and David Meenagh 2020

All rights reserved. No part of this publication may be reproduced, stored in a retrieval system or transmitted in any form or by any means, electronic, mechanical or photocopying, recording, or otherwise without the prior permission of the publisher.

Published by
Edward Elgar Publishing Limited
The Lypiatts
15 Lansdown Road
Cheltenham
Glos GL50 2JA
UK

Edward Elgar Publishing, Inc.
William Pratt House
9 Dewey Court
Northampton
Massachusetts 01060
USA

A catalogue record for this book
is available from the British Library

Library of Congress Control Number: 2020948671

This book is available electronically in the **Elgar**online
Economics subject collection
http://dx.doi.org/10.4337/9781839103070

MIX
Paper from
responsible sources
FSC
www.fsc.org   FSC® C013056

ISBN 978 1 83910 306 3 (cased)
ISBN 978 1 83910 307 0 (eBook)
ISBN 978 1 83910 308 7 (paperback)

Printed and bound in Great Britain by TJ Books Limited, Padstow, Cornwall

Contents

Preface

This book is a sequel to the one I wrote in the run-up to the Brexit referendum *Should Britain Leave the EU? An Economic Analysis of a Troubled Relationship* (second edition). Fortunately, the result of the referendum was a decision to leave the EU, which is now being implemented after a decisive election returned Boris Johnson's government, which pledged to carry Brexit out. Now we must deal with the issues of what must be done to make Britain's future outside the EU a success. This is the subject matter of this book. These issues have been complicated by the coronavirus crisis, a further challenge to policy.

In the research work that lies behind this book I have been lucky to be part of a brilliant team of co-authors and fellow researchers – in particular, Mai Le, David Meenagh (who co-wrote the Appendix to Chapter 5 of this book) and Yongdeng Xu. Together we and our co-workers have been working on the models necessary to get an understanding of the economic processes affecting our trade, our regulations and the macroeconomy. I have tried to write in a way quite accessible to non-modellers, and yet give a clear account of the ideas and practices we have followed.

I would also like to thank the team at Edward Elgar Publishing, led by Alex Pettifer, who have once more come to my aid in the endeavour to write on these central policy issues of our time. They have helped me to overcome the technical challenges of making this work presentable and so I hope readable.

Last, but of course not least, I thank my wife Rosie for putting up with it all; I dedicate this book to her.

1. Introduction and summary

In this book, the themes of my earlier book, *Should Britain Leave the EU?* (Minford et al., 2015), are pulled together to discuss how we should follow up with post-Brexit policies, now that Brexit has finally taken place. 'What should Britain do, having left the EU?' This is what this book aims to answer. As before, I will rely heavily on research that my co-authors and I have done, mostly now in Cardiff over the last 20 years, building on earlier work in Liverpool over the previous 20.

The earlier book explored the gains from free trade that could be made by abandoning the EU protectionism that dictated our commercial policies. In this book, I flesh out how free-trade policies will reshape the economy, and, in turn, how other policies should be adapted to this new world.

Another set of gains will come from a new regulative approach, replacing the interventionist regulation of the EU, with its redistributive and socializing aims; continental law, where one can only do what is explicitly permitted, lends itself to prescriptive regulation, whereas common law, where one can do whatever is not forbidden, lends itself to independent innovation. We will set out a way of modelling these gains, and the policies that can reinforce them.

What we will see is that there is also a need for new policies across other areas – notably, fiscal policy, including tax structure, and monetary policy, including the new much-vexed role of 'prudential' controls. This is especially urgent after the coronavirus crisis. Then too we must look at how public money is spent: too much spending is not 'joined up' with good information and hence ineffective. In an age of huge information flows and easy communications, spending should facilitate and strengthen private choices at local level within the community.

We have an unparalleled opportunity to remould our policies across the board in order to set the economy on a new course with the ability Brexit gives us to rethink policy that has increasingly been dominated by EU institutions, which as our previous book argued, were not economically well structured.

This book starts with trade and regulation, these being the two key areas of EU control we will be dismantling. These involve the detailed settings of the tax and regulative system, which act directly on the market behaviour of firms and households at the 'micro' level; we go on to consider the structure of the UK's whole tax system to complete this microanalysis, affecting the supply side of the economy. We then move on to consider how 'macro' policy should be set in the future: that is, the management of demand in the economy. We review fiscal and monetary policy in the current crisis and go on from there to consider how they should evolve in the post-Brexit, post-COVID-19 economy. In what follows I give an overview of the book's arguments.

PART I: RESTORING BRITAIN'S COMPETITIVENESS THROUGH FREE TRADE AND REFORMS OF THE TAX AND REGULATORY SYSTEM

Chapter 2 on Trade

At the heart of the EU's powers is the control of commercial policy – that is, tariffs and non-tariff barriers, including standards set so as to exclude supplies from certain other countries, notably the US, and also anti-dumping duties and quotas on supplies from particular countries. Commercial policy is designed to create large trade barriers against non-EU competitors, both in agriculture and manufacturing. In services such as financial, which are not so important to the EU as industries , EU commercial policy is fairly liberal, though national governments remain highly restrictive of foreign competition, including from the rest of the EU; it is only recently that the single EU market has been extended to some services, so restraining national protection against the rest of the EU. UK service industries operate worldwide and so are little affected by this mainly national protectionism. UK service prices are therefore set by international competition at world prices; this will not change when we leave the EU.

However, UK goods prices are currently dominated by EU prices, which are higher than world prices by the percentage of trade barriers, which are estimated in our research and elsewhere at around 20% for both food and manufactures. Leaving the EU and negotiating wide free trade agreements (FTAs) with non-EU suppliers so that they gain free access to our markets will bring UK prices down 20% to world levels – this, which is equivalent in its effects to unilateral free trade, will, according to the

Global Trade Analysis Project (GTAP) model now used by the Treasury, bring gains of 4% of gross domestic product (GDP) through better prices to consumers and competition-led rises in productivity by UK producers. According to Cardiff research, the gain would be double, while simply abolishing half the EU protection would bring in the same gain. This is our preferred (cautious) assumption. Astonishingly, the Treasury, in its latest report, assumes this gain to be only 0.2% of GDP, on the grounds that this policy is barely carried out – totally contrary to announced government policy.

The Treasury's gloom does not stop there. It also assumes that large trade barriers will spring up along the UK–EU border after Brexit, for two reasons. First, the EU will refuse to recognize that our exports satisfy their standards, and we will do the same; second, it and we will institute border checks that artificially delay our trade in both directions at the border. However, both these things are illegal under World Trade Organization (WTO) rules, to which both we and the EU remain entirely committed. Under the GTAP model these new barriers cost us over 5% of GDP. Yet, these costs are entirely illusory.

The Treasury, on its own admission, has a bad track record on its trade modelling. Before the referendum it produced equivalent estimates of the Brexit costs to the UK due to trade; it did so using 'gravity' equations instead of a full model of world trade with implied Brexit impacts through all channels. Since then, it has conceded that its gravity equation methods were faulty because they did not compute the full Brexit effects on, but rather took as constant, aspects of the economy such as wages and other home costs that would also simultaneously change with Brexit. Hence, their move to adopt the GTAP model.

Unfortunately, in changing their model they did not change their determination to find negative effects from Brexit via absurdly pessimistic assumptions, such as we have detailed above. When we replace these assumptions about a Brexit on WTO rules, we find the GTAP model gives a net gain of 2.6% of GDP. Our own Cardiff World Trade Model on our assumptions gives a gain of 4% of GDP.

Chapter 3 on Regulation

Regulation is the second major area controlled by the EU, through its powers to regulate the Single Market. It exercises these powers according to a 'social market' philosophy. A nation state has the power to tax/subsidize, and it can use this power to redistribute income to the less well-off.

However, the EU has no tax powers because national governments have been unwilling to pass them over to it, even partially. Therefore, to achieve social objectives of a redistributive nature, the EU uses regulation; examples are labour market 'rights' that are essentially subsidies to workers paid for by implicit employment taxes on firms.

Thus, one finds that labour market regulation is a series of subsidies to workers and trade unions, paid for by firms. The effects on the economy can be assessed according to the labour tax equivalent, plus the direct implied transfer to worker-households. It was largely to carry out this assessment that my research team built the 'Liverpool Model' of the UK economy; this was the first macro-model of the UK to have a full 'supply side', designed to compute the effects of tax and regulation on the economy's potential output. In an Appendix to this chapter, we take a backward look at how the supply-side reforms of the 1980s' Thatcher governments affected the economy.

The EU's regulation extends beyond the labour market to three other main areas. The first is general product market standard setting, which as we have seen is related to setting trade barriers. The general aim of standards is to benefit the main producer industries of the EU. Thus, these industry lobbies have essentially had the power to legislate what suited them. As Adam Smith noted centuries ago, such power in the hands of business is likely to be anti-competitive; one notices that the EU Competition Directorate takes its most stringent actions against foreign, often US, companies – such as Apple, Google and Facebook. One can in principle assess this producer regulation as the equivalent of endowed monopoly power, like a consumer tax. In practice, estimates of this are hard to make, other than via the direct effect of the trade barrier; this barrier also puts an effective limit on the extent to which home industries can raise prices. So, we have not estimated any additional effect of regulation as such via this route.

The second area beyond labour is finance, a service where the EU has shown a strong desire to control activity, although, or perhaps because, the biggest EU finance industry has been in the UK. It has intervened with highly prescriptive regulations in this major UK industry, in a way that is extremely unpopular among its practitioners – supposedly to protect consumers. These regulations have given rise to an army of 'compliance' executives, but while this has raised costs substantially, gains to consumers have been unclear; in other major markets, such as the US, similar interventionism has been avoided. We can leave on one side here the new regulations on banks associated with the financial crisis, which we discuss later in the context of monetary policy. In the UK this was mostly self-inflicted.

Finally, there is the rest of the economy: (1) the environment and climate where the EU has regulated strongly to force the adoption of non-fossil-based energy; and (2) the regulation of technology, especially in agriculture and pharmaceuticals, where the EU has given primacy to the precautionary principle, and held back technological innovation. The main effect in the first has been to raise energy costs instead of primarily focusing on developing new technology that would be most effective in the long term and least costly in the short term. With regard to technology, EU regulation has held back innovation.

In all these areas we propose estimates of the cost to the UK economy. Overall, we suggest a cost of 6% of GDP, of which we suggest 2% can be rolled back. In a parallel piece of analysis of the Thatcher reform programme, discussed in the Appendix to this chapter, we find comparable gains, suggesting that this order of magnitude is indeed feasible.

To these gains we add that of avoiding uncontrolled EU unskilled immigration, which the UK taxpayer has subsidized by around 20% per migrant, costing 0.2% of GDP, mainly paid by poorer UK taxpayers. On top of this we eliminate the annual net payment to the EU budget, 0.6% of GDP.

Chapter 4 on Tax Reform

The UK needs a tax system for the twenty-first century that delivers large and stable revenues without penalizing either savings or incentives for successful people. We show that this can be done by rebasing the income tax system on consumption and cutting marginal tax rates in the process.

A good tax system is one that creates the minimum damage to everyone's incentives to work and save – the 'Ramsey Principle' – consistently with financing government spending and achieving the necessary income redistribution. This is achieved by taxes (1) that are 'flat' (i.e., the same proportional rate) across people of all incomes (the popularly known 'flat tax'); (2) that are flat across commodities of all sorts ('tax neutrality'); and (3) that are flat across time. This last means that the tax rate is constant over present and future consumption; it implies both that tax should be levied on consumption and that the tax rate should be planned to be constant under forecast conditions ('tax smoothing').

Taxes can be cut without being balanced by simultaneous cuts in spending because extra work and less avoidance create an offsetting recovery in revenue (the Laffer effects) and because higher growth generates more future revenue. This is an important implication of tax smoothing. A UK flat tax on consumption would bring the imputed rent on owner-occupied housing into the tax base and would allow the standard rate of income tax to be cut cautiously to a 15% flat tax rate on consumption, thereafter being cut further in stages as the growth effect rolled in. Such tax reform would be popular since there would be no losers, no cutback in public spending programmes and many gainers, not the least of them the UK economy.

PART II: SUPPORTING BRITAIN'S ECONOMY THROUGH FISCAL AND MONETARY POLICY

Chapters 5 and 6 on Fiscal and Monetary Policy

We first explain how central banks have made a complete mess of monetary policy over the financial crisis. Their first major mistake was to stimulate a big credit boom in the 2000s, which was the main cause of the crisis situation, through overleveraged banks. Second, they permitted the Lehman liquidity crisis, by allowing Lehman to go bust instead of getting it taken over, with liquidity pumped into the banking system. It was this bust that precipitated the crisis proper. Third, they stymied bank credit growth post-crisis by draconian bank regulation just when credit growth was needed for recovery.

Fourth, they flooded markets with quantitative easing (QE, the aggressive buying by central banks of bonds and other assets by printing money), which has created large distortions in financial markets. There is now evidence that this last episode, zero interest rates and QE, have damaged competition and new industrial entry by subsidizing capital to large firms. This has created a market structure argument for 'normalizing monetary policy' besides arguments from monetary policy itself, to the effect that we need to make it effective again.

To restore monetary policy effectiveness, we need interest rates to rise back to normal, well away from the zero lower bound where they still are. The only way for policy to deliver this is via a fiscal expansion. This can be Brexit related, focused on using the much-improved public finance situation to deliver tax cuts and growth-supporting spending. We set out full fiscal and debt projections over the next two decades, which show that this can be done while debt remains under control in the long term.

Finally, we set out new work on how monetary policy can, once it recovers effectiveness, more effectively target nominal GDP than simply inflation. Such a new central bank-targeting set-up, backed up by a fiscal commitment to prevent a zero lower bound, will deliver a much more stable economy, making the whole programme of direct control of bank balance sheets and 'prudential' intervention redundant.

Chapters 7 and 8 on Fiscal Rules, Public Spending Reform and the New Fiscal Strategy for Growth

As we move out of the coronavirus crisis, fiscal policy needs to be guided by long-term rules about government solvency; these project the future long-term public sector balance sheet, rather than imposing short-term rule-of-thumb constraints on current budgets or borrowing. Owing to interest rates being close to zero, the long-run cost of the huge COVID debt is rather small. This means that post-COVID and post-Brexit, the government can continue to be bold in fiscal policy, making tax cuts and spending on infrastructure that creates growth, which in turn will create the extra revenue to pay for it. We show how a programme of continued borrowing in the order of £100 billion a year is affordable on UK post-Brexit projections, after the COVID package has been financed and the economy has recovered from the crisis.

If one examines UK public spending, it is a massive share of GDP, at around 40%, and yet its effectiveness is constantly in dispute, whether in health, education, policing, or almost any area of public involvement. Yet, the technical ability of central agencies to communicate and use information efficiently now exists, and with it the ability to coordinate decentralized efforts. Ideas for devolving areas downwards to communities could therefore be widely explored, following the work of Elinor Ostrom on public 'commons'. Some practical experiments appear to have been made in social care by health boards in the context of the internal market for healthcare, and in education via work on competition with the public sector. There is scope for a rethink of how competition works in railways and between modes (road vs rail), as well as revisiting road pricing, where Singapore is a living example of how it can be done.

Barriers to growth: reducing government obstacles to entrepreneurship and entrepreneurial innovation
The ultimate job for government is to remove the obstacles placed by tax and regulatory policies on business formation by entrepreneurs. The

very existence of government is an invitation to rent-seeking lobbyists for regulations that favour their special interests. Because there is then no general lobby for potential businesses opposing such open-ended interference, this lobbying process is constantly adding to the regulative environment in ways that impede business. It is this accretion that has to be periodically scraped away by a process of deregulation that prioritizes the business freedom on which our growth and prosperity depend.

In this context, we showcase recent research on how the Thatcher revolution in tax and regulation kickstarted productivity growth. An issue that comes up repeatedly is the 'productivity puzzle', according to which productivity growth has slowed down markedly in recent years. However, it seems most likely that this is simply mismeasurement of the effects of rapidly growing digital productivity.

The North–South policy challenge

A major challenge is to bring the North's income up to the level of that of London and the South. As many people have pointed out, a good start would be to improve the infrastructure of the North, which has lagged behind that in the South, especially in terms of transport. HS2 has become controversial because of cost overruns, but the main argument for it is not faster journeys, which is where the cost–benefit has focused, but simply that it is the most economical way to produce the extra North–South journey and freight capacity needed because of increased congestion on road and rail. Doing this by expanding the current rail capacity would be expensively disruptive. HS3 should go ahead quickly as well, together with the improvements promised in the Northern Powerhouse programme.

However, the policies that will work to generate growth in the North are the same as those that will generate growth across the whole economy. Our new Regional Model finds that general policies cutting taxes and regulative intervention have the biggest proportional effects in the North, because there is less congestion there in resources, both labour and land. There is therefore no contradiction between stimulating the economy as a whole via supply-side policies and 'levelling up'.

THE DOGS THAT DO NOT BARK IN THIS BOOK

This book does not deal with a number of topics that are widely discussed in the public debate: namely, climate change, the issue of ageing and the 'demographic time bomb', a detailed regulation agenda, and how to ensure multinational firms pay their 'fair share' of existing taxes. Let me explain why.

In all these issues I believe the 'solutions' lie with individual actions within free markets, once the government has set out its actions in areas where it controls the levers. So, climate change is now something that ordinary households have clear concerns about: investors are therefore responding with new technologies to satisfy them by delivering the services they want in a way that improves the climate. One sees this in the rapid development of battery technology, of electric cars, and the increasing use of hydrogen. Top-down government action and controls look increasingly redundant and potentially counterproductive.

Ageing and demographics again are areas where private action is vigorous. The population is getting older because they are healthier for longer; as a result, they plan to work for longer and possibly in different ways or activities as they age. Similarly, population growth across the planet will adapt to household preferences – as women participate more in work, household incomes rise and living space becomes more expensive, they have fewer children and population growth falls. Government action to control demographics has rarely been effective, anyway; it is also undesirable in people's choices.

I spend a fair amount of space in this book discussing the costs of bad regulative intervention. But I have nothing much to say about 'good regulation', because, again, markets should basically be left alone to create their own standards for products and services via the competitive process dominated by consumer preferences. Government's role is to let markets do this job by getting out of the way, unless there is some clear social abuse. If government has information about the effects of consumer choices, then it should publish this effectively so that people make better-informed choices. In a free society, people must be left to choose their own lives.

The same applies to questions of 'what industrial structure will emerge' from the COVID crisis. This will be determined by consumer preferences interacting with new technologies and their costs. At this point we really cannot know what these will be. Will there be less travel? Will people telecommute much more and offices be used much less? To such questions, markets will provide answers in time; government should keep out of the way as resources are redeployed. Its role is to support the economy via general fiscal/monetary policies and good supply-side policies to support growth.

I have dealt in this book with how the tax system should be reformed to collect the needed revenue with the least damaging effects on growth. The tax base should be as broad as possible – consumption fits the bill – and the marginal tax rates as low as possible. What about those multinationals that brazenly avoid corporation taxes by 'filtering' their profits through tax havens? This activity has always been a predictable response to the foolish attempt by governments to tax mobile capital. It has revealed that corporation tax is a poor tax base. It is only paid by domestic firms that have no escape. Better to abolish this tax, and the complicated superstructure of double tax agreements; replace it with the consumption tax advocated in Chapter 4. As for the tech firms that provide 'free services' in return for our data, truly this is consumption via barter, much like the implied rental income from home ownership. Their value could be included similarly in consumption via imputation. Then there would be no need to single out 'tech firms' for a controversial 'digital tax'.

This book focuses narrowly on how the government should use the levers it has: in trade barriers like tariffs and regulative discrimination, in taxation, in regulation, and in fiscal and monetary policies to support the economy on the demand side, these other policies all being operative on the supply side. These policies set the general framework within which the UK's free markets can satisfy consumers' needs. A government that can get this framework right is doing the best it can for the British economy. It should firmly resist the temptation to do more – let markets and consumers do the rest.

REFERENCE

Minford, P., with S. Gupta, V.P.M. Le, V. Mahambare and Y. Xu (2015), *Should Britain Leave the EU? An Economic Analysis of a Troubled Relationship*, 2nd edition, Cheltenham, UK and Northampton, MA, USA: Edward Elgar Publishing.

PART I

Restoring Britain's competitiveness through free trade and reforms of the tax and regulatory system

2. The trade effects of Brexit on the UK economy

I was astonished during late 2015 to discover that most economists in the UK favoured staying in the EU on the basis of what appeared to be neo-protectionist arguments derived from recent 'gravity-related' trade thinking. In late additions to the second edition of my book *Should the UK Leave the EU?* (Minford et al., 2015), I pointed out that the gravity modelling was of a partial equilibrium nature and that attempts hitherto made to turn it into general equilibrium were misconceived. It soon became apparent that my professional colleagues were not going to take any notice of these points; and, indeed, the Treasury economists promptly enlisted help from the London School of Economics (LSE) gravity trade group in developing the gravity-based case for retaining existing trade links with the EU, regardless of the costs of its well-known protectionism.

I begin in the first half of the chapter with comments on the various rival 'gravity' approaches. I then go on in the second half to set out the quantitative analysis we reached on Brexit, using our own models and realistic Brexit policy assumptions. In the Appendix, I set out the statistical work we carried out to test the various approaches and show that the gravity approaches are rejected on UK trade data.

GRAVITY TRADE MODELS AND BREXIT: A REVIEW

At the heart of the Brexit debate there is a fundamental disagreement about how trade works and affects the economy. In the last few years, debate has raged over whether EU trade arrangements are beneficial, in particular to the UK. The EU is a customs union and so erects trade barriers around its Single Market where economic activity is regulated according to EU rules. The welfare effects of a customs union have always been controversial. According to classical trade theory, global welfare is reduced compared with free trade, as is the average welfare of citizens inside the customs union; however, one country's citizens may gain from the union if it is a net exporter to others in the union, as then its terms of trade gain may offset the losses experienced by its consumers (Meade, 1955). However, in recent times, a new line of reasoning has become popular among trade economists: this 'gravity model' (e.g., Costinot and Rodríguez-Clare, 2014) regards trade as an outcrop of internal trade, the only difference being that it crosses borders. Otherwise, it grows naturally due to the specialization and division of labour within neighbouring markets. Viewed through the lens of the gravity model, a customs union merely makes official what is already a fact of neighbourly inter-trade. Other sorts of trade, with more distant markets, grow analogously, but more weakly, the greater the distance; size of distant markets may make up for their distance to some extent, because they are a 'neighbourhood' that naturally leads to inter-trade. 'Gravity' in trade creation can be thought of as a function of distance and size. In this view of trade, it makes no sense to put obstacles in the way of trade with close neighbours such as the EU in the hope of boosting trade with distant markets via new trade agreements that lower trade costs. The disruption from the former will reduce welfare, while the gains from the latter will be small, simply because the reduced trade costs will have little effect in switching demand from existing products in the presence of weak and imperfect competition.

Before we go further into the technicalities of different models and calculations of trade policy effects, it is worth spending a little thought on what light the history and structure of UK trade can throw on the matter. For centuries, the UK has been regarded as the archetype of a 'trading nation' in that its great trading companies, such as the East India Company, sought out trading opportunities around the world and in the process founded the British Empire, with trading links all over the world. European neighbouring countries had little to do with it, other than the Dutch with whose Indies' trading fleets the UK fought several wars, settled by the Treaty of Westminster in 1674. In recent years, UK trade has been dominated by services, whose weightlessness implies a total lack of 'gravity'; furthermore, the containerization of goods transport has brought shipping costs down to almost trivial levels. The role of gravity, viz. distance × size, seems, on the face of it, to be small in UK trade. As for European trade, despite high EU tariffs against non-EU suppliers, the share of EU trade (imports plus exports) in UK trade has never gone above 25% of UK gross domestic product (GDP). Currently, it is running at 20% against around 30% with the non-EU world, so UK trade with the EU is about 40% of all its trade, despite massive trade barriers (around

20% in both food and manufactures) against non-EU countries. It does not look as if gravity has much to do with it all, certainly European gravity. It is perhaps not a surprise that classical trade theory, with its strong relevance to far-flung UK and other Northern European (Swedish/Dutch) trade, was developed by British and Northern European economists such as Ricardo, Heckscher and Ohlin, while the more recent gravity theory has mainly been developed by economists based in the US or continental Europe where distant trade plays a minor role in GDP. Compare the UK with a country like the Czech Republic with limited trading activity other than with the EU by which it is surrounded; 80% of its trade is with the EU, reflecting its quite different trade opportunities, which are indeed naturally describable by gravity. It would certainly be unsurprising if our tests of UK trade rejected the gravity model – as we will see in the Appendix in which we set out our formal tests of the models, it does.

Before that, we review the various attempts that have been made by different groups of economists, using different approaches, to evaluate the trade effects of Brexit.

'GRAVITY MODEL' ESTIMATES OF BREXIT TRADE EFFECTS

Clearly, these two models, the classical and the gravity models, are different and so may well have different welfare implications. However, while trade economists have recently tended to favour the gravity model over the classical, there has been no convincing empirical test of the two models as overall predictors of the data. Gravity modellers do point to the Tinbergen (1962) gravity regressions as evidence in favour of the gravity model: these are statistical correlations between the size of two countries' GDPs and their distance from each other on the one hand, and the size of their trade on the other. However, these regressions have long been familiar to trade economists, and classical trade models too can generate trade data in line with these regressions. Thus, we face here an 'identification' problem: two models can both generate the same data – at least, that would be the claim of their proponents. We need an empirical test that can discriminate powerfully between the two models – we will develop this in the Appendix.

Plainly, one has to use the underlying model (i.e., one in which all the interactions within trade and the economy are allowed for) to calculate policy effects, since these work through all the channels of the model; one surely, so we would say, cannot use the Tinbergen and related regressions, since these are simply correlations and associations generated by the model, and are not causal. So, we would argue that we must uncover the true model – and this requires a test, to be shown later.

HM TREASURY 2016 CALCULATIONS

However, gravity theorists of trade have argued that one can use these associations directly to assess the effects of Brexit. The most notable example of this was the Treasury's report in 2016 (HM Government, 2016). For its calculations, it directly used associations (correlations) between (1) trade and GDP and trade agreements as with the EU; (2) trade and foreign direct investment (FDI); and (3) FDI and productivity. It applied regression estimates of agreement effects on trade in gravity trade equations (1), to obtain the effects on UK–EU trade by commodity. It then used the trade/FDI regressions (2) to obtain the effects of this reduced trade on FDI. Finally, it inputs these FDI reductions into equations at (3) to obtain the productivity effects. Finally, it fed the productivity into exogenous potential output, and thence into a macro model of the UK, NiGEM (ibid.).

There are many detailed criticisms that have been made of these calculations. These include the fact that in the trade regressions, the effects of EU membership on many diverse economies are averaged to get the UK effects. Critiques include Burrage (2016) and Gudgin (2017), and Economists for Free Trade (2018) which includes pieces by Blake, Dowd, Congdon and me.

But there is a more fundamental and quite devastating criticism of this method, which is that it is based on 'partial equilibrium' relationships that take the aggregate environment, such as UK GDP, prices, wages and supplies of factor inputs, as given. This assumption cannot be made when a major policy change like Brexit trade arrangements is involved. This change will simultaneously affect all parts of the economy: sector production, investment/FDI, goods/services prices, factor supplies and prices such as wages, land rents and returns on capital. Calculating these 'general equilibrium' effects can only be done by a model that includes them all interactively, as is done in general 'macro models' or in trade models that contain the same relationships but usually without dynamics (i.e., lags in adjustment and expectations), 'computable general equilibrium' (CGE) models.

After exposure to this last criticism, the Treasury and Civil Service finally switched in 2018 to a full general equilibrium approach, using a well-known model developed at Purdue University, Indiana – the Global Trade Analysis Project (GTAP) model. This moved the discussion towards the issue of what sort of CGE model should be used. To decide this issue, one must set CGE models of differing specifications against each other and test them against the data, preferably with a powerfully discriminating test. We have attempted to advance this discussion by constructing a moderate-sized CGE model of the basic 'classical' type alongside one of a 'gravity' type, in which the key gravity mechanisms are added to the classical model. So far, we have completed tests of both against UK trade data; tests against US and Chinese data are ongoing. We have deferred discussion of this quite complicated procedure to the Appendix.

However, not all those groups estimating Brexit effects have conceded that the partial equilibrium method is wrong. Several notable UK centres – LSE Centre for Economic Performance (LSE-CEP), National Institute of Economic and Social Research (NIESR) and the Sussex Trade Policy Observatory – have continued to promulgate their estimates based on this method. We review their methods and estimates in more detail next.

OTHER UK GROUPS' MODELLING STRATEGIES AND CALCULATIONS

Three modelling groups have published full accounts of their calculations: LSE-CEP, NIESR and Sussex Trade Policy Observatory. We consider their methods in turn.

LSE-CEP

This group gives details of their various exercises in Breinlich et al. (2016). In their main calculations, they follow a 'reduced-form approach' similar to the Treasury's original one (HM Government, 2016), and find results that are similar or larger; in fact, in an Appendix reviewing the Treasury work, they argue it is 'too cautious' because it leaves out larger 'dynamic effects' on FDI and productivity. Our comments on this are the same as for the Treasury's, set out above – such a partial equilibrium analysis does not capture the causal mechanisms at work.

Breinlich et al. (2016) use, as an alternative approach, a static CGE model, which they provide detail about in Technical Appendix 3. There they explain that their method is to solve the Armington demand equations (a set of consumer-based demand relationships) using an elasticity of trade to tariff-induced price changes. With this assumed elasticity they can solve these equations for implied trade, expenditures, outputs and welfare. They get much smaller estimates from this model than from the reduced-form approach above, which they make it clear they prefer – wrongly, we would say for reasons given.

However, the main problem with their 'state-of-the-art' model is the key assumption of a general elasticity of trade response, whatever the shocks to the model. We know from CGE models that different shocks work through different channels to produce different trade elasticities. Thus, tariffs on food, for example, have pronounced effects on land prices, which in turn affect costs and outputs in other sectors, whereas tariffs on manufactures have effects through wage costs. The implied elasticities of trade (which aggregate all these different channels) are different. Indeed, some will be zero, according to the classical model, which alone passes the test of matching UK trade data, as we will explain below. For example, UK tariffs on EU goods will have no effect once UK tariffs on non-EU goods have gone due to new free trade agreements (FTAs). The only way of estimating these various elasticities is to simulate effects in a full, empirically satisfactory, CGE model.

NIESR (Hantsche, Kara and Young, 2019)

Essentially, this NIESR study (its latest, made in November 2018) follows the same procedure as the Treasury's original study (HM Government, 2016) discussed above. There is no attempt at a general equilibrium analysis of trade. The NIESR findings are therefore similar to that of the Treasury study. For the case of an EU FTA, GDP is projected to fall by 3.9%; for a World Trade Organization (WTO) exit, by 5.5%. Our critique of this NIESR partial equilibrium approach is, accordingly, the same as of the Treasury's above: by using these partial relationships, the NIESR has ignored the indirect effects on trade via factor markets, prices and wages. Its results are therefore fallacious.

Sussex Trade Policy Observatory (Gasiorek, Serwicka and Smith, 2019)

The approach taken by this Sussex University group is unapologetically partial equilibrium and limited to the manufacturing sector. They esti-mate at a highly disaggregated level the effects of different trade policies on manufacturing prices, exports, imports and output. In these estimates, they hold UK aggregate GDP, prices and wages constant; hence, no attempt is made at a general equilibrium analysis, nor at estimates of effects on GDP.

The pessimistic nature of these results can be gauged from those for the WTO-rules Brexit case (but where no trade deals are done). For the manufacturing sector, when all subsectors are added up, they obtain:

Manufacturing: exports −19.5%; imports −7.3%; output −5.5%; prices +5.0%

Even with an FTA with the EU and rolling over the EU's 67 FTAs with other countries, the figures are little different, with manufacturing output, for example, falling by 4%. They do not model a policy of free trade (zero tariffs and other trade barriers) with the Rest of the World (RoW), which would have reduced prices at least.

The problem with this study is the same as that of the Treasury's original study (HM Government, 2016) in that it makes no attempt to allow for general equilibrium effects via GDP, or home wages and prices. These effects are substantial even if one is only concerned with manufacturing sectors, because resources will shift as factor prices change, and manufacturing output and productivity will react to these shifts. The main gains to GDP through CGE analysis of free trade with the RoW come through falling home manufacturing and food prices driving down home costs, raising home productivity in previously protected sectors and shifting resources to more productive sectors. Unfortunately, this failing makes the Sussex Trade Policy Observatory estimates largely valueless from a general equilibrium perspective.

THE TREASURY'S CGE MODEL CALCULATIONS SINCE THE REFERENDUM

After discarding use of its widely criticized 'gravity-like' model used in the initial 'Project Fear' Referendum forecasts, the Treasury has now adopted use of a CGE model (GTAP from Purdue University) that is similar to the World Trade Model used by Cardiff University in modelling general equilibrium behaviour.

In this comment we ignore the migration calculations made by the Treasury that imply large extra costs; however, these costs are based on the assumption that the flow of migrants will be abruptly cut off. As it is now government policy that skilled migrants will be flexibly treated under a points-based immigration system, while unskilled migrants will be allowed in temporarily but without access to state benefits, this assumption is the opposite of the truth.

While this more recent Treasury work adopts a full CGE approach and so avoids the criticisms we advanced above of its and its allies' partial equilibrium approach, there remain two main difficulties with what it has done. First, the CGE model it has used adopts a 'weak gravity' model, which we find does not fit the UK trade facts; we will discuss this issue further in the Appendix. Second, and perhaps a lot more damaging, it adopts policy assumptions that are highly questionable; we will show that when these are altered to reflect more realistic assumptions, the evaluation of Brexit turns from negative on UK welfare to strongly positive.

Based on the latest Treasury report (HM Government, 2018a) and its Technical Reference Paper (HM Government, 2018b), the assumptions are flawed in three fundamental ways:

1. They assume *de minimis* benefits for the UK economy from future free trade agreements with non-EU countries:
   a. Only a 0.2% boost to GDP is forecast vs an estimate for Australia on the same model of more than 5% from its 30 years of trade liberalization.
   b. It gets this by assuming the following:
      i. Quite low estimates of EU non-tariff barriers (NTBs) (based on econometric work) at around 7% for goods (other estimates suggest 16%). For services, it assumes UK NTBs after leaving the EU would be 15% (our estimate is zero as the UK has a liberal regime for services trade).
      ii. Only half of the goods NTBs can be abolished, and only one-third of the services NTBs, leading the resulting NTBs to fall, as shown in Table 2.1
      iii. Adding these abolishable NTBs to the average tariffs on goods gives a total eliminable of 8% on goods (average tariffs 4%); and 5% on services (no tariffs here).
   c. Under GTAP, if these were abolished via FTAs that achieved the same barrier reduction on our imports as unilateral free trade, the gain would be 1.6% of GDP:

Table 2.1   *Summary of UK–EU trade weighted tariffs, by sector,*
                 in the modelled no deal scenario, compared to today's
                 arrangements

	Compared to Today's Arrangements (% Change)	
	Tariff on UK Imports from the EU (%)	Tariff on EU Imports from the UK (%)
Chemicals, pharmaceuticals, rubber and plastics	2	2
Machinery, electronics and aerospace	1	1
Motor vehicles and parts	9	8
Other manufacturing	3	3
Agri-food	20	20
Networks	0	1

Source: HM Government (2018b), Table 2.A.

    i.   However, in practice, the Treasury assumes only around half these gains would be achieved by FTAs, because of limited coverage. This brings the gain down to 0.8% of GDP.

   ii.   Then, the Treasury assumes that only one-quarter of this programme will occur as it is 'under development' – see paragraph 76 from Section 3.3.1 in HM Government (2018b):

> The Government's approach to agreements between the UK and prospective trade partners is currently being developed. In this illustrative and indicative approach representing ambitions agreements including but not limited to FTAs, it is estimated that under the central ambitious case, 25% of the actionable goods and services barriers might be reduced. These are applied in all the modelled EU exit scenarios. As set out in section 2.3.3 of the analysis document [HM Government, 2018a], the analysis does not model any constraints that the Government's policy could impose on future UK-RoW agreements. (HM Government, 2018b, p. 25)

This reduces the gain to the headline 0.2% of GDP.

2.   Turning to UK-EU trade, high border costs are assumed for the processing of customs declarations, rules of origin certificates and goods inspections. This reflects a lack of understanding of how modern computerized, pre-declared border procedures work:

Table 2.2   *Summary of estimates of changes to UK–EU NTBs by sector compared to today's arrangement*

	Compared to Today's Arrangements (% Change)				
	Modelled No Deal	Modelled Average FTA	Modelled EEA-type	Modelled White Paper	Modelled White Paper with 50% NTB Sensitivity
All goods	+10 (+6 to +15)	+8 (+5 to +11)	+5 (+3 to +7)	+1 (0 to +1)	+4
All services	+11 (+4 to +18)	+9 (+3 to +14)	+2 (+1 to +3)	+6 (+2 to +10)	+7

Note: Central estimates and ranges in brackets. Estimates are rounded to the nearest %. Owing to rounding, narrow ranges (less than 1%) are not distinguishable in the table.
EEA = European Economic Area
Source: HM Government (2018b), Table 2.D.

    a.   Typical actual costs of modern procedures are well below 1% and the Swiss customs authority reports costs of 0.1%.

    b.   Inspections are intelligence led and a rarity (typically only 1–3% of shipments). They often require only confirmation of computerized documentation and can take place away from the border. These Treasury-assumed but unrealistic costs across goods and services give rise to a loss of 1.8% of GDP.

3.   Imaginary high compliance costs on UK-EU trade are assumed for exporters/importers to meet hypothetical new non-tariff barriers springing up immediately after Brexit. These NTBs (Table 2.2) include the border costs discussed in the previous paragraph:

    a.   This is based on the mistaken belief that the EU will suddenly determine that UK exporters do not meet product standards – despite over 20 years of shared rules and standards.

    b.   Such behaviour would be illegal under WTO anti-discrimination rules that require importers from all countries to be treated the same – that is, a UK importer cannot be required to meet a standard that is not required of, say, a US importer or indeed an internal producer from the EU. In other words, they must be existing EU standards – which we meet.

    c.   The Treasury fails to understand how trade actually works – that is, that is. each exporter makes independent decisions to set their product configurations given the attractiveness of export markets. Hence, even as standards change in the future, exporters will make sure, in their own commercial interests, that their goods continue to meet these standards, as occurs throughout the world with export trade.

In reply to our criticism of these estimates, the Treasury evades the point, as shown in the following quotation from HM Government (2018b), Section 2.7.2, paragraph 63:

> Rather than model NTBs with the EU, the Economists for Free Trade Study assumes no additional NTBs. They argue that given the UK's current regulatory alignment with the EU, any attempt to impose trade barriers would be illegal under WTO rules. The OBR [Office for Budget Responsibility] notes that 'this appears to be based on Economists for Free Trade's interpretation of the WTO's MFN [most-favoured-nation] requirements. But most trade experts interpret these rules as meaning that the EU would be forced to impose the same NTBs that the rest of the world currently faces, unless the UK and EU sign a trade deal to lessen them. (HM Government, 2018b, p. 20)

That is, simply saying that the WTO rules may not be implemented. Note that the EU imposes standards that the UK currently meets; these are 'the same EU standards that the rest of the world currently faces'. These standards, of course, act as NTBs to countries such as the US that cannot meet them.

The combined total effect of these assumptions is that – beginning with product standards and regulations identical to those of the EU – it would be as if the UK faced an EU tariff-equivalent cost on goods and services combined of around 14.5% (of which only 4.5% is actual goods tariffs) if trading under WTO rules. This is about three-quarters of the effective tariff actually faced by the US, which, in fact, trades with the EU under WTO rules.

When these flawed assumptions are fed into the Treasury's GTAP model, it forecasts a reduction to UK GDP of 7.7% (Figure 2.1). This is amazing considering that total EU trade accounts for only 12% of total UK GDP and only about 40% of this trade is exports that could be affected by such EU restrictions.

Table 2.3 compares the result of the Treasury model results with the estimated results that would be obtained from the same model if assumptions that were more reasonable than those used by the Treasury were fed into the model.

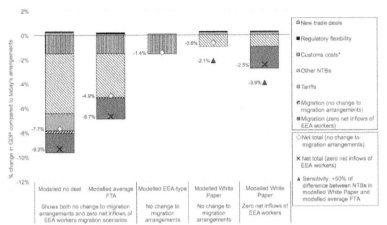

Note: Central estimates only. *NTB estimates for the modelled no deal and modelled average FTA scenarios are derived from econometric modelling, which does not isolate individual NTB components. Customs costs for these scenarios are shown illustratively in line with the modelled European Economic Area (EEA)-type scenario estimates. This considers trade, migration and regulatory flexibility effects. There are a number of external assessments comparable to the modelled no deal, average FTA and EEA-type scenarios. The government's estimates sit within the range of external estimates, noting that key differences between studies relate primarily to assumptions on changes to trade costs and how economic models simulate the economy's adjustment to these. Few studies have sought to model the stated government policy.
Source: HM Government (2018a), Figure E.3.

Figure 2.1   *Decomposition of total impacts on GDP compared to today's arrangements for the illustrative no change to migration arrangements and zero net inflows of EEA workers scenarios*

It should be noted that, due to the use of econometric estimates, the new EU trade barriers now assumed are lower than the judgements used in an earlier draft of the report (Civil Service, 2018), and indeed have been roughly halved. But the response of the UK part of model in the new report (HM Government, 2018a) has been raised (more than doubled) to compensate and give a similar-sized hit to UK GDP from WTO and FTA scenarios. This alteration of the GTAP model the Treasury is using is puzzling and suggests that outsiders need to have access to discover just why these changes have been made as well as their empirical justification.

It should be also noted that in separate work – see the Appendix – we have tested different model variations in our own Cardiff World Trade

Model and found that the most accurate model is closest to the perfect competition classical version, while gravity model versions are rejected – with the fullest gravity version strongly rejected.

Table 2.3   *Trade effects under Brexit scenarios according to GTAP-type model used by Whitehall*

	Whitehall Assumptions		Alternative Assumptions	
	WTO	Canada+	WTO	Canada+
Tariffs	4.5		4.5	
Effect on GDP	*−1.4*		*−1.4*	
New standards	5.5	5.0		
Effect on GDP	−4.4	*−3.5*		
New customs costs	4.8	4.2		
Effect on GDP	−1.8	*−1.4*		
Total tariff equivalent (%)	14.5	9.2	4.5	
Total effect on GDP (% of GDP)	*−7.7*	*−4.9*	*−1.4*	
FTAs with rest of world		+0.2		+4.0*
Effect on GDP (% of GDP)				
All trade effects on GDP (% of GDP)	*−7.5*	*−4.7*	*+2.6*	*+4.0*

Note: Trade barriers expressed as % tariff equivalent; effect on GDP shown as % of GDP in italics. Figures show author's calculations based on Treasury sources cited in the text. *Assumes all EU protection of food and manufactures (20% average on each) eliminated via FTAs.

CARDIFF WORLD TRADE MODEL CALCULATIONS OF BREXIT EFFECTS ON UK WELFARE

We noted in Table 2.3 that under the Treasury's GTAP model, if realistic Brexit assumptions are inputted along the lines we argued above are appropriate, then according to that model, there would be a welfare gain to the UK from Brexit due to the trade effects of 2.6% of GDP under a WTO-rules exit, or 4% under an exit with a Canada-plus EU FTA.

If we apply the same assumptions to the Cardiff World Trade Model, which we show in the Appendix passes our empirical tests against UK trade data, the gains are larger. If we assume that only 10% of the existing EU 20% protection of food and manufactures is abolished, then the gain to UK GDP is 4%, mainly via higher productivity, while consumer prices fall 8%; if we assume that the full 20% protection is abolished, these numbers double. This is true both under the WTO-rules exit and Canada-plus EU FTA regardless; the reason these are the same is that once the UK has driven UK prices to world prices via FTAs with the non-EU world, it makes no difference what EU FTA we strike. EU producers, like our own home consumers and producers, can only sell and buy in our markets at world prices; EU trade barriers will simply be passed on to EU consumers, while UK trade barriers must be absorbed by EU suppliers. Paradoxically, this implies that the UK Treasury can levy tariffs on the EU and gain at the EU's expense, while the EU can only raise any tariff revenue it gets from UK imports from its own consumers.

It is worth explaining how these results come about. A key effect of agricultural protection is a large rise in the price of agricultural land. This acts as the base price for alternative use of all land that gets planning permission to be used in other sectors. Hence, it raises costs of production across the whole economy. The non-traded sector contracts as prices rise.

BROADER ISSUES OF INTERNATIONAL TRADE POLICY

This chapter has focused on the technical implications of different UK bilateral trade policies. But behind these lies the important international issue of the world trading system and its WTO-based rules. Both the system and the rules are under attack from their two biggest members, the US and China. The US, led currently by President Trump but with some general US consensus, has attacked the WTO as putting the US at a disadvantage, with others exploiting its free trade approach; it is particularly incensed by China's protectionism and pirating of US technology by state-led 'deals' for US firms entering China, which mandate technology handover. The US originally welcomed Chinese membership of the WTO on the assumption that it would lead to Chinese policies of free market openness. This was originally forthcoming under Deng Xiaoping's leadership but since Xi Jingping became leader, China has embraced a nationalistic policy of protectionism and national champions in 'key parts' of the economy; this has gone hand in hand with an aggressive expansionism in foreign policy.

Into this cauldron of confrontation the coronavirus crisis has now arrived, with huge recrimination between the US and China over the origins of the infection and policies towards it. A major consequence of the crisis is likely to be a large-scale shift away from outsourcing to distant supply chain providers because of both risks of future lockdowns and possible trade friction disputes.

The UK's interests in strong trade links dictate that our policies should aim to buttress WTO authority and rules and that we should oppose attempts by both China and the US to disrupt the system and disobey the rules. In these efforts we will need to build a wide coalition of countries with similar interests to ours in an open world trading system. These countries can be found in the Trans-Pacific Partnership (TPP) group in Asia, including Australia, New Zealand and Japan. As advocated by Singham and Tylecote (2019), the UK should forthwith apply to join this group, along with other FTAs with non-EU countries, including the US and China. As they argue, the UK should become the voice pushing for wide agreement on new liberal regulative standards for goods and services. Increasingly, international standards bodies are taking over the process of building international cooperation on standards, which in turn become the building blocks against trade discrimination, as outlawed in general under WTO rules. Hence, the UK has an important role in international diplomacy in pursuing a stronger world trading order.

CONCLUSIONS

In this chapter we have reviewed the wide range of work analysing the trade effects of Brexit under a variety of trade policies. We have shown that the trade models closest to the UK data have weak or non-existent 'gravity' mechanisms within them and that these models predict substantial gains from striking free trade agreements with non-EU countries, regardless of what agreement is struck with the EU. We have also shown that when reasonable assumptions about policy are fed into models with stronger gravity elements, there are fairly large gains to be made by general free trade together with a basic FTA with the EU. The UK trade policies should therefore be the pursuit of not simply an agreement with the EU to keep zero barriers but also simultaneously a wide range of free trade agreements around the world – most of all with the US, free trade with whom would bring most of the gains from general free trade with the non-EU world. Finally, the UK has a strong interest in an open world trading system under WTO rules and widely agreed international standards and it should use its best efforts to promote this via a coalition of countries with similar interests.

APPENDIX: CLASSICAL OR GRAVITY? WHICH TRADE MODEL BEST MATCHES THE UK FACTS?

In this Appendix we explain how the main classical and gravity trade models differ and examine the empirical evidence bearing on whether UK trade is governed by a classical model or by a gravity model, using annual data from 1965 to 2015 and the method of indirect inference, which has very large power in this application. The gravity model here differs from the classical model in assuming imperfect competition and a positive effect of total trade on productivity. We found that the classical model passed the test comfortably, and that the gravity model also passed it but at a rather lower level of probability, although as the test power was raised it was rejected. The two models' policy implications are similar.

The Workings of Trade Models

Gravity model

During the referendum debate and since, the Remain side has relied on a 'consensus' of trade economists in favour of the 'gravity model'. The Treasury's case against Brexit was based on this, as has been the work at the LSE on which the Treasury relied for much advice (Breinlich et al., 2016).

A gravity model is in principle a full model of the economy open to international trade, investment and borrowing. It regards trade as an outcrop of internal trade, the only difference being that it crosses borders (e.g., Costinot and Rodríguez-Clare, 2014). Otherwise, trade grows naturally due to the specialization and division of labour within neighbouring markets. Viewed through the lens of the gravity model, a customs union merely makes official what is already a fact of neighbourly inter-trade. Other sorts of trade, with more distant markets, grow analogously, but more weakly, the greater the distance; size of distant markets may make up for their distance to some extent because they are a 'neighbourhood' that naturally leads to inter-trade. 'Gravity' in trade creation can be thought of as a function of distance and size. In this view of trade, it makes no sense to put obstacles in the way of trade with close neighbours, such as the EU, in the hope of boosting trade with distant markets via new trade agreements that lower trade costs. The disruption from the former will reduce welfare, while the gains from the latter will be small, simply because the reduced trade costs will have little effect in switching demand from existing products in the presence of weak and imperfect competition.

Under this model, trade is determined largely by the forces of demand, from neighbours wanting imports and from others modified by the factor of distance – due to transport costs and border costs; competition is rather limited, highly 'imperfect', and prices are set by producers as a mark-up on costs, so they move rather little. Once demand has determined trade and the production to meet it, FDI and associated innovation follow it, boosting productivity. In short, while supply is important in this gravity approach, supply is largely determined by the forces of demand.

Because it is hard to break into new and distant markets, it makes sense in this approach to support existing markets. Hence, leaving the EU will damage existing markets' demand, so reducing trade and so reducing supply and productivity via falling FDI and innovation. Reducing trade barriers with the rest of the world will only weakly substitute for this loss of demand by stimulating more demand there.

Even though the EU protects its markets via trade barriers, this, on the gravity view, is good for the UK because it raises demand for our exports within the EU. Hence, this school of thought is in favour of EU protectionism – it could be called 'neo-protectionist'. In general, free trade, according to the gravity approach, is something that must be evaluated case by case based on its effects on demand for UK products and so the supply side of the economy.

Proponents of this gravity approach claim that it is supported by the 'facts' – consisting of many estimated relationships between exports and the GDP of the demanding countries, adjusted for distance. However, as already explained, we need to allow for a possible problem: that the rival classical model also generates these relationships. Indeed, it has routinely been thought by proponents of this rival model that such gravity equations, first estimated by Tinbergen (1962) and well known since, would be implied by the model.

The classical model

This classical model was developed by the great trade theorists of the past two centuries – starting with Ricardo (1817) – and pursued in much empirical work based on it. The fact that these ideas come from a long tradition of thinking does not, of course, mean that they are thereby wrong because they are 'old'. We have also witnessed an earlier major reversal of classical thought, the Keynesian Revolution, which has now been largely ditched in favour of a return to classical principles.

The classical model assumes high competition across world markets, with world prices being the same across the world subject to transport costs and trade barriers; there is free entry into all industries so that prices equal average costs. Capital flows freely across borders in the modern world version, but each country has largely fixed supplies of other factors – namely, unskilled labour, skilled labour and land. In this model, supply forces such as the supply factors and their productivity determine the size of a country's different sectors. The resulting income is then spent according to home demands and the surplus of supply over demand is then exported, the deficit imported in each sector. The model is silent on the allocation of demand to imports and home goods and on the allocation of exports to different foreign markets. However, it would be normal to add on some such allocative model of demand on top of the basic structure.

Thus, it can be seen that the causal structure of the classical model is quite different from that of gravity thinking. In the classical model, supply determines the essential structure of trade; demand adjusts to be consistent with this. In the gravity approach, demand determines the structure of trade and in turn forces supply to adjust to this.

How Do Gravity Modellers Implement Their Model?

You might think from this account of the gravity approach that you would expect to see – at the Treasury and at the LSE – a full CGE model of the UK's economy, trade and foreign investment, complete with final demands, markets for labour and capital, and market clearing, including balance of payments equilibrium. But this is not what you will find. Instead, there will be some equations for bilateral trade in a lot of different goods with different countries in which GDP at home and in foreign countries figure together with relative prices; then another lot of equations for different countries relating FDI to trade; then yet another lot of equations for UK industries relating productivity to FDI. The 'model' generates results by computing what under the first set of equations a trade regime change would do to trade; then this is 'fed' into the second set of equations relating FDI to total trade; finally, the FDI effect is fed into the last set of equations relating FDI to productivity. The resulting estimate of the productivity effect of the trade regime change is then put into a model of the economy. This procedure can be found in the Treasury's long-term assessment of the effects of Brexit (HM Government, 2016). The LSE pursues a broadly similar methodology.

What we have is one set of empirical associations between trade and trade regimes; another set of associations between trade and FDI; then another set of associations between FDI and productivity. Only at the last stage when all this has been computed from these associations is a model brought in, where productivity is inputted into a standard 'macro' model in which the origins of trade and its interactions around the economy are not included. While all the empirical associations are based on data, they do not tell us what the causal origins of these associations are. There could be reverse causation (FDI could cause trade or productivity cause FDI; trade regimes could have been caused by closer trade), or simultaneous causation by a third factor (better policies could have led simultaneously to more trade, more FDI and more productivity). Association, as is well known, does not imply causation.

There is therefore a serious question of identification – that is, interpretation of what causal processes are driving these associations. One would like the gravity modellers to write out a complete system of causal equations that they believe in and set them side by side with a rival system such as the classical model. Then we could check which of these two systems comes closest to implying all these associations we observe – more precisely since this debate is about Brexit, implying the associations we find for specifically UK trade and the UK economy – that is, the 'UK trade facts'.

But during the Brexit referendum debate there never was in existence at the Treasury (see Annexes to HM Government, 2016) and the LSE (see pp. 12–23 in Breinlich et al., 2016) any such complete gravity trade model linking all goods, labour, capital and land markets into one (UK) 'economy' linked to the rest of the world. Nor has anyone in either place asked whether such a model would fit the UK trade facts; it simply has not occurred to them to build the model or to ask it this question.

Gravity and Classical Trade Models – Tests, Checks and Policy Implications

To make some progress on these issues, we spent a year doing work of this sort on a gravity model of the UK. We took a full classical trade/economy model and adjusted it for gravity assumptions: first, imperfect competition; and second, an effect from total trade to productivity (via FDI). What we found is detailed in Minford and Xu (2018).

We found by testing these models against the full array of associations found in the data that the gravity model is statistically rejected while the classical model survives the test. As this is the first time to our knowledge that trade models have been tested in this way, it is of interest to show a few details of how this test was conducted. Formally, it is an indirect inference test in which the facts of UK trade relationships are summarized in some way, the 'auxiliary model', and the trade models to be tested are then simulated repeatedly to create alternative sample histories from each of which these summary facts are extracted. This creates a joint distribution of these facts, which can be used to assess the probability of the trade model generating the actually observed facts. If the probability lies in the test's tail (which we set at the usual 5% level), the model is rejected.

A first question concerns the power of this test, which we assess by a Monte Carlo experiment,[1] hypothetically falsifying to an increasing extent some 'true model' similar to one of our models here. We create many samples from the true model; we then disturb the true parameters by + or − x% alternately and see how many of these samples reject our falsified model. The left-hand column of Table A2.1 shows this x% 'general mis-specification' and the next column the rejection rate. It can be seen that this rejection rate that measures the power of the test rises sharply to virtually 100% once mis-specification reaches only 3%.

Figure A2.1 shows a comparison of the actual data for a variety of variables whose joint behaviour needs to be matched by the model simulated data for the model to pass the test. Side by side with the actual data, we show the model simulated data averaged across all simulations. If the data for each variable is similar to the average simulation, then the data's joint behaviour will match the simulated joint behaviour on average.

Table A2.2 shows the probability of the data coming from the model (p-value) under our most powerful form of the Wald test.

The Policy Implications for Brexit of the Two Models

But we made a finding that is perhaps more important for policy: when we put the assumption of free trade into the gravity model, it produces the same answer for the effects on UK welfare and GDP as the classical model. What this means is that, had gravity modellers used the true underlying causal model of trade and the economy, together with the full free trade assumptions about policy, to compute the effects of Brexit they would have come to a strongly positive conclusion about post-Brexit economics, as we did. The reason is clear: even in the gravity model, general free trade lowers consumer prices and stimulates resource movement to the more productive sectors.

Table A2.1   Power of II Wald test: classical model assumed as true using final (most powerful) form of the test

% Mis-specified	Indirect Inference Test
True	5.0
1	40.5
3	99.9
5	100.0
7	100.0
10	100.0
15	100.0
20	100.0

Source: Minford and Xu (2018), Table 9.

Table A2.2   II Wald test results using the most powerful form of the test

	P-value
Classical trade model	0.0904
Gravity model	0.0350

Source: Minford and Xu (2018), Table 10.

Later Modelling Developments

The Treasury released no replies to our criticisms of these gravity-equation-based methods, nor indeed did any of the other modellers using similar methods. Rather the contrary, they happily allowed sympathetic outside commentators like the Institute of Fiscal Studies (Emmerson et al., 2016) to trumpet abroad the fact that our work was an 'outlier', without drawing attention to the differences of modelling method or of assumptions where the method was similar. In fact, there

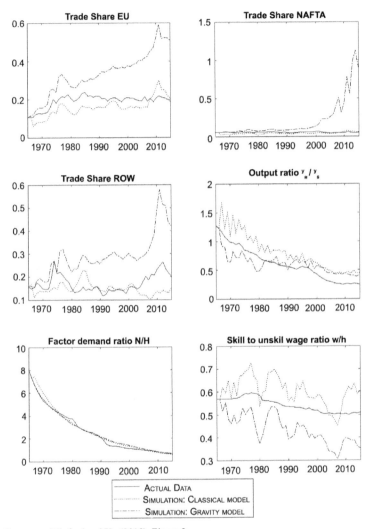

Source: Minford and Xu (2018), Figure 2.

Figure A2.1 Actual and average of simulated data

has always been a spread of economists' analyses, giving the lie to the implication that we were the only economists who thought Brexit would or could have a positive trade effect on the economy.

Thus, our group was not the only one to find that Brexit would have a positive long-term trade effect under favourable policy assumptions. Another was Open Europe (Booth et al., 2015), which used the GTAP model from Purdue University, Indiana, a well-known internationally developed CGE model of world trade. It is a model of all countries, grouped into smaller groups, usually around 50, and of all goods and services sectors, usually around 40. Its equations are derived from trade theory, and the equilibrium in each market of supply and demand. Furthermore, as noted by Whyman and Petresku (2017), other studies finding negative Brexit effects used a variety of damaging assumptions that had nothing to do with trade, such as short-term uncertainty, migration and regulation.

However, more significantly, the Treasury and the rest of the UK Civil Service have now collectively abandoned the gravity-equations methods described above and so in terms of method have now joined us in using a general equilibrium model of trade, as evidenced by the Cross-Whitehall (Civil Service, 2018) project. Thus, had they shared our policy assumptions, they too would have come up with similarly positive assessments of the trade effects, as we have shown in this chapter.

NOTE

1. Monte Carlo simulations are used to model the probability of different outcomes in a process that cannot easily be predicted due to the intervention of random variables. It is a technique used to understand the impact of risk and uncertainty in prediction and forecasting models.

REFERENCES

Booth, S., C. Howarth and M. Persson et al. (2015), *What If...? The Consequences, Challenges and Opportunities Facing Britain Outside EU: Open Europe Report 03/2015*, accessed 27 August 2020 at http://europas-krisen.zdf.de/media/downloads/Brexit/150507-Open-Europe-What-If-Report-Final-Digital-Copy.pdf.

Breinlich, H., S. Dhingra and G. Ottaviano et al. (2016), *BREXIT 2016: Policy Analysis from the Centre for Economic Performance*, accessed 27 August 2020 at http://cep.lse.ac.uk/pubs/download/brexit08_book.pdf.

Burrage, M. (2016), *Myth and Paradox of the Single Market: How the Trade Benefits of EU Membership Have Been Mis-sold*, London: CIVITAS, accessed

27 August 2020 at http://www.civitas.org.uk/content/files/mythandparadox
.pdf.

Civil Service (2018), *EU Exit Analysis: Cross-Whitehall Briefing* [PowerPoint],
accessed 27 August 2020 at https://www.parliament.uk/documents/commons
-committees/Exiting-the-European-Union/17-19/Cross-Whitehall-briefing/
EU-Exit-Analysis-Cross-Whitehall-Briefing.pdf.

Costinot, A. and A. Rodríguez-Clare (2014), 'Trade theory with numbers:
quantifying the consequences of globalization', in G. Gopinath, E. Helpman
and K. Rogoff (eds), *Handbook of International Economics*, Vol. 4, Oxford:
North-Holland, pp. 197–261.

Economists for Free Trade (2018), 'The critique of project fear', accessed
27 August 2020 at https://www.economistsforfreetrade.com/publication/the
-critique-of-project-fear.

Emmerson, C., P. Johnson, I. Mitchell and D. Philips (2016), *IFS Report 116:
Brexit and the UK's Public Finances*, Institute of Fiscal Studies, May 2016,
accessed 27 August 2020 at https://www.ifs.org.uk/uploads/publications/
comms/r116.pdf.

Gasiorek, M., I. Serwicka and A. Smith (2019), 'Which manufacturing industries
and sectors are most vulnerable to Brexit?', *The World Economy*, **42** (1),
21–56.

Gudgin, G. (2017), 'Defying gravity: a critique of estimates of the economics
of Brexit', *Policyexchange.org*, 26 July, accessed 27 August 2020 at https://
policyexchange.org.uk/publication/defying-gravity-a-critique-of-estimates-of
-the-economic-impact-of-brexit.

Hantzsche, A., A. Kara and G. Young (2019), 'Prospects for the UK economy',
NIESR Economic Review, 247, F12–F46.

HM Government (2016), *HM Treasury Analysis: The Long-term Economic Impact
of EU Membership and the Alternatives*, April 2016, Cm 9260, accessed 27
August 2020 at https://assets.publishing.service.gov.uk/government/uploads/
system/uploads/attachment_data/file/517415/treasury_analysis_economic
_impact_of_eu_membership_web.pdf.

HM Government (2018a), *EU Exit: Long-term Economic Analysis*, November
2018, Cm 9742, accessed 27 August 2020 at https://assets.publishing.service
.gov.uk/government/uploads/system/uploads/attachment_data/file/760484/28
_November_EU_Exit_-_Long-term_economic_analysis__1_.pdf.

HM Government (2018b), *EU Exit: Long-term Economic Analysis: Technical
Reference Paper*, November 2018, accessed 27 August 2020 at https://assets
.publishing.service.gov.uk/government/uploads/system/uploads/attachment
_data/file/759763/28_November_EU_Exit_Long-Term_Economic_Analysis
_Technical_Reference_Paper.PDF.

Meade, J.E. (1955), *The Theory of Customs Unions*, Amsterdam: North-Holland.

Minford, P., with S. Gupta, V.P.M. Le, V. Mahambare and Y. Xu (2015), *Should
Britain Leave the EU? An Economic Analysis of a Troubled Relationship*,
2nd edition, Cheltenham, UK and Northampton, MA, USA: Edward Elgar
Publishing.

Minford, P. and Y. Xu (2018), 'Classical or gravity: which trade model best
matches the UK facts?' *Open Economies Review*, **29** (3), 579–611, accessed

27 August 2020 at http://orca.cf.ac.uk/108158/2/10.1007%252Fs11079-017
-9470-z.pdf.

Ricardo, D. (1817), *On the Principles of Political Economy and Taxation*,
London: John Murray.

Singham, S. and R. Tylecote (2019), 'Plan A+: creating a prosperous post-Brexit
Britain', *Discussion Paper No 95+*, Institute of Economic Affairs, September
2019.

Tinbergen, J. (1962). *Shaping the World Economy: Suggestions for an
International Economic Policy*, New York: Twentieth Century Fund.

Whyman, P.B. and A.I. Petresku (2017), *The Economics of Brexit – A Cost–
Benefit Analysis of the UK's Economic Relationship with the EU*, Basingstoke:
Palgrave Macmillan.

3.   The costs of EU regulation[1]

The power of the EU to regulate product and labour markets comes from the Single Market arrangements of the mid-1980s. These gave powers to the Commission, with the agreement of the EU governing council of member states under qualified majority voting (QMV), to issue directives in these matters. The greatest irony about this arrangement is that it was forced through the EU by a coalition of the UK and Germany; Margaret Thatcher's UK government of the time was particularly enthusiastic about what it saw as a spreading of competition across all EU markets; Jacques Delors, the EU Commission president, used this enthusiasm cleverly to get the measure through against much socialist resistance from other countries.

The UK government was naive in thinking that the measure would work to spread competition. What we now know is that Jacques Delors promised the resisting governments a socialist arrangement to 'compensate' for the pressures from the Single Market. No sooner was the Single Market adopted than he announced the creation of a Social Chapter of the Treaties that would ensure the Single Market satisfied social objectives. While the UK negotiated an opt-out from the Social Chapter, outraged at what it saw as a betrayal of the Single Market vision, in due course Tony Blair's Labour government of 1997 gave away this opt-out, apparently in a bid to promote an image of the UK as 'pro-European', though also tacitly agreeing with much of the social agenda: Blairite Labour, like politicians such as Yvette Cooper, has always supported the social agenda, as facilitating Labour's regulative socializing agenda 'from above' it avoids the need for Labour to expend political capital on the moves. But, in any case, even with the opt-out, the Single Market's health and safety provisions were used to put a cap on UK working hours, a major restriction on the workings of the labour market. Once the opt-out went, a great raft of labour market intervention in the UK followed; these included Transfer of Undertakings (Protection of Employment) Regulations of 2006 (TUPE, giving unions protection of their previous arrangements under privatization), enhanced maternity and new paternity rights, rights for part-timers equivalent to those for full-timers, equal pay for women and 'minorities', and rights for unions and workers to 'full consultations' before factories could be closed or redundancies made. The interventions have so far stopped short of imposing on the UK the full gamut of union-friendly arrangements usual on the continent but there could be no certainty they would not be forced in over time. QMV implied that the UK was potentially outvoted on all issues involving the Single Market where the continent follows a different philosophy. QMV does not so far apply to harmonization of social security and social protection policies; however, one can have no confidence that it will not eventually be extended to cover these too.

In what follows, we review first the labour market regulations where the most intrusive general interventions from the EU occur. Second, we look at product market regulation where there is a particularly strong threat to the major UK markets in the City as well as a general tendency to push up costs to 'harmonize' standards across the EU; such harmonization effectively is set to reduce competition with the EU's dominant producers in each industry.

LABOUR MARKET REGULATION IN THE EU

It is clear that labour market institutions in the rest of the EU are hostile to job creation. This is not just our view here but also that of the Organisation for Economic Co-operation and Development (OECD). It is also well evidenced by the high levels of unemployment throughout the EU for some years – of course, recently exacerbated by the eurozone crisis.

Thus, the OECD has for years conducted surveys of the extent of labour market 'protection', by which it means barriers to hiring and firing workers. These surveys (where the index runs from 0 to 6 – the higher the value the higher the burden) are based largely on responses by employers to questionnaires about the burdens they see imposed by regulation. The 2013 pre-Brexit survey is reproduced in Table 3.1. It can be seen that the UK is substantially less protectionist than other EU countries, in spite of the general pressure from Social Chapter principles. Nevertheless, it is more protectionist than the US and this arguably reflects this pressure to date. In a recent report to the prime minister (Beecroft, 2012), the venture capitalist Adrian Beecroft pointed out that in a wide variety of ways, the UK was failing to give businesses enough freedom in their labour relations and that this was contributing to slowing the growth of jobs in the UK. Fortunately, in spite of this, UK jobs growth was satisfactory up to 2016, though we remained below full employment and participation in the labour market of specific groups of workers, such as women, the young, older workers and disabled workers, remained disappointing.

What remained a particular concern is how far this pressure could go in the future, had we stayed in the EU. The EU Social Chapter favours strong powers for unions as well as invasive regulations on hiring and firing. Were the UK to be pressured into reaching the sort of environment prevailing in some other parts of the EU, the results would be dramatic. In an exercise to compute these possibilities using the Liverpool Model of the UK (for details of the model see Marwaha et al., 1984), we carried out simulations of what they might do, which are reproduced in Table 3.2.

It can be seen that these are large costs, even in the least-cost scenario with its cost at 9% of gross domestic product (GDP) and 10% on unemployment. The high-cost scenario is obviously hugely damaging, at 20% of GDP and an unquantifiable rise in unemployment.

What exactly was the effect of EU membership and specifically the introduction of the Social Chapter on the UK? We can use the general OECD series on employment protection to give us an idea. From 1985 to 1999, the value was 1.032; from 2000 to 2012 it rose and stayed at 1.198, almost a 20% rise. This can be associated with the effects of new measures brought in after the Social Chapter became binding on the UK in 1997. In 2013, the coalition government acted on the Beecroft Report and brought in a package of measures on issues where the Social Chapter was not binding that reduced the value back to 1.032. What we can see from this is that we have so far been able to maintain a reasonably liberal order in the labour market in spite of the Social Chapter. However, the situation is constantly shifting, with new decisions by the European Court and new directives from the Commission. So far, it seems we have been able to offset one set of regulative measures with another later set of liberalizing ones. Nevertheless, the Social Chapter can be seen in itself to have raised the index by nearly 20%. The measures involved are listed in the Beecroft Report – they include TUPE, which protected union employees against dismissal by the new company after a privatization, extended rights for temporary workers, provisions for extended consultation over closures and dismissals, and numerous directives on worker rights of all sorts. They do not include self-inflicted interventions like the introduction of the minimum wage.

Table 3.2 showing effects of different degrees of EU intervention is just an illustration of the possibilities. Clearly, some parts have already been enacted. But the key point is that, as we look forward and try to

Table 3.1   *OECD measures of labour market intervention from 0*
                   (least restrictions) to 6 (most restrictions)

	Protection of Permanent Workers Against Individual and Collective Dismissals (EPRC)	Protection of Permanent Workers Against (Individual) Dismissal (EPR)	Specific Requirements for Collective Dismissal (EPC)	Regulation on Temporary Forms of Employment (EPT)
Austria	2.44	2.12	3.25	2.17
Belgium	2.95	2.08	5.13	2.42
Denmark	2.32	2.10	2.88	1.79
Estonia	2.07	1.74	2.88	3.04
Finland	2.17	2.38	1.63	1.88
France	2.82	2.60	3.38	3.75
Germany	2.98	2.72	3.63	1.75
Greece	2.41	2.07	3.25	2.92
Hungary	2.07	1.45	3.63	2.00
Ireland	2.07	1.50	3.50	1.21
Luxembourg	2.74	2.28	3.88	3.83
Netherlands	2.94	2.84	3.19	1.17
Norway	2.31	2.23	2.50	3.42
Poland	2.39	2.20	2.88	2.33
Portugal	2.69	3.01	1.88	2.33
Slovak Republic	2.26	1.81	3.38	2.42
Slovenia	2.67	2.39	3.38	2.50
Spain	2.28	1.95	3.13	3.17
Sweden	2.52	2.52	2.50	1.17
Switzerland	2.10	1.50	3.63	1.38
United Kingdom	1.62	1.12	2.88	0.54
United States	1.17	0.49	2.88	0.33
OECD unweighted average	2.29	2.04	2.91	2.08

Note: Data refer to 1 January 2013 for OECD countries and Latvia, 1 January 2012
for other countries. Only version 3 indicators (indicator abbreviations in brackets) are
reported.
Source: OECD Employment Protection Database, 2013 update.

Table 3.2   *The effects on UK output and unemployment of EU-style social measures*

Social Measures		
I. A minimum wage		
where wage is:	(a) 50% of male median	(b) 2/3 of average
Long term effects on:		
Output (%)	−1.5	−5.0
Unemployment:		
% of labour force	+1.8	+5.0
Million	+0.5	+1.4
II. Union power simulation		
Union power rises:	(a) to mid-1980s level	(b) to 1980 level
Long term effects on:		
Output (%)	−3.0	−5.8
Unemployment:		
% of labour force	+1.3	+4.3
Million	+0.4	+1.3
III. Rise in the social cost burden on employers:	(a) by 20% of wages	(b) by 60% of wages
Long term effects on:		
Output (%)	−4.4	−11.0
Unemployment:		
% of labour force	+3.0	+18.0
IV. Combination of minimum wages, union power rise, and higher social cost burdens on employers (combination of I–III, (a) and (b))		
	Least	Most
Long term effects on:		
Output (%)	−9.0	−20.0
Unemployment:		
% of labour force	+10.0	(Extreme value)
Million	+3.0	(Extreme value)

Source: Minford (1998), p. 200 – simulations based on Liverpool Model of the UK (Marwaha et al. (1984).

predict how 'ever-closer union' might work out for us with our traditions
of relatively free markets, we cannot have much confidence in what
could happen within the EU, given that our partners, who can dominate
the agenda via QMV, have quite different labour market institutions and
approaches that can be briefly summarized as being corporatist or socialist ('social democratic', favouring regulation rather than ownership as the
means to achieve social objectives).

PRODUCT MARKET REGULATION

The original idea for the regulation of EU product markets was that each
country would have its own regulations and from the resulting regulative
competition would emerge some convergence towards a more general
and effective system. This idea did not last long in the face of demands
from industry protagonists for a 'level playing field'; leading firms in
each sector feared that firms in other countries could be advantaged by
a different, less intrusive regulatory system. There could be a 'race to
the bottom' in regulatory laxness; dominant firms would then face easier
entry from rivals. They lobbied for a high and equal level of regulation,
a 'level playing field'; standards would be 'raised' across the industry,
preventing competitors from entering the market with different products.

Measuring this excess regulation is difficult. Fortunately, as in the case
of labour market regulation, the OECD has devoted a lot of resources to
surveys measuring the regulatory barriers created by governments. In
Table 3.3, we reproduce the OECD's overall product market regulation
index.

It is interesting to see that the level of regulatory burdens recorded by
business has gone down throughout the EU since 1998. Nevertheless, in
the UK it has hardly changed, falling very slightly over the period to 2008
and dropping a bit further since then. It remains below every other EU
country, other than the Netherlands, which has had a pro-business culture
for a long time.

This index is made up of a host of sub-indices; the UK's relative attrac-
tiveness to business is widely spread across the three main categories of
sub-index: state control, barriers to entrepreneurship and barriers to trade
and investment. Thus, it would seem that EU membership has not obviously damaged the UK's performance in business regulation and that the
Single Market is in this respect functioning reasonably well. One caveat
is in order: if the regulations are written to please the dominant producers
in each product area, they might well express satisfaction even if the

Table 3.3   *Product market regulation – OECD measures*

	Product Market Regulation			
	1998	2003	2008	2013
Austria	2.12	1.61	1.37	1.19
Belgium	2.30	1.64	1.52	1.39
Czech Republic	2.64	1.88	1.50	1.39
Denmark	1.66	1.48	1.35	1.22
Estonia	–	–	1.37	1.29
Finland	1.94	1.49	1.34	1.29
France	2.38	1.77	1.52	1.47
Germany	2.23	1.80	1.41	1.29
Greece	2.75	2.51	2.21	1.74
Hungary	2.66	2.11	1.54	1.33
Iceland	2.03	1.62	1.48	1.50
Italy	2.36	1.80	1.49	1.26
Luxembourg	–	1.60	1.44	1.46
Netherlands	1.82	1.49	0.96	0.92
Norway	1.87	1.56	1.54	1.46
Poland	3.19	2.42	2.04	1.65
Portugal	2.59	2.12	1.69	1.29
Slovak Republic	–	2.17	1.61	1.33
Slovenia	–	–	1.89	1.70
Spain	2.39	1.79	1.59	1.44
Sweden	1.89	1.50	1.61	1.52
Switzerland	2.49	1.99	1.55	1.50
United Kingdom	1.32	1.09	1.20	1.08
United States	1.50	1.30	1.11	–

Source: OECD.

consumer is less well served. However, as there is no survey of consumer opinion, and indeed it would be hard for consumers to judge such industrial matters, we have no evidence on this point. What evidence we have from industry therefore does support the idea that harmonized regulation works well.

The Fraser Institute in Canada, in cooperation with other free market think tanks around the world, compiles another measure of business regulation burdens; here, the index is on a scale of 0–10 and as it rises the burden is falling (Table 3.4).

Table 3.4   Business regulation index, Fraser Institute

	Business Regulation Index
Austria	6.2
Belgium	6.2
Denmark	6.9
France	6.2
Germany	6.6
Ireland	7.0
Italy	5.5
Luxembourg	7.1
Netherlands	6.9
Spain	6.0
US	6.7
UK	7.0

Source: Gwartney, Lawson and Hall (2012).

The picture is not very different in its current level from that given by the OECD surveys. Again, the UK is close to the top of the ranking and apparently none the worse for being in the EU. However, the Institute has measured UK levels of business regulation since 2000 when it was 8.17. Since then it has dropped to 7.6 in 2005, fallen further to 6.8 in 2010, and only recently in 2012 picked up slightly to 7.0. These scores out of 10 are not terrible, but, overall, we observe a drop of around 14% over the period – again, we are likely to be seeing here the effect of increased regulative activity by the EU since the UK governments of Blair, Brown and Cameron were not in favour of increased business regulation.

We should note that because the rest of the EU is in general more burdensome in its regulations, this remains a pressure point from the UK's viewpoint, in that other countries may not be averse to the UK introducing greater regulatory burdens to avoid its having a competitive advantage. This temptation for other EU countries, burdened by high regulatory costs, to raise UK costs in order to reduce the effects on their own competitiveness is endemic.

One area of regulation where a visible and substantial cost is being incurred is the EU's climate change agenda on renewables. This is estimated to be costing the economy, mainly directly charged for in fuel bills, some 2% of GDP (Congdon, 2014). Renewable energy in the UK is high cost, even more so than elsewhere because of the vagaries of wind and sun; its costs are compounded by the need to back up these energy supplies with more reliable sources. Whatever the merits of the climate change agenda, these high costs indicate that there are more cost-effective ways to pursue it.

Another area where UK interests are seriously threatened by EU regulation is the City of London. Here the overall regulation has now been placed in EU hands since 2014. Apart from placing a cap on staff bonuses and proposing a Financial Transactions Tax (still being fought over), the EU regulators have not yet moved on the new framework. Tim Congdon (2014) has recently written on the outlook for this and concluded that it constitutes a serious threat to the City's future functioning. The problem with this area of business is that the rest of the EU have been mostly hostile to UK- and US-style finance and banking, which does not prevail anywhere else in the EU, apart from the Netherlands, Ireland and Luxembourg to a moderate extent. Plainly, the City of London is a major UK industry, contributing some 10% of UK GDP; for it to be regulated by a hostile EU process is a matter of great concern.

We cannot cost this threat in any sensible way. In our table of potential costs due to regulation we may think of this threat as contributing to the higher end of the cost range. Essentially, the UK faces in respect of this regulation, as with labour market and product market regulation, a substantial range of uncertainty, given the existence of QMV. The other countries of the EU share an approach to these matters that is generally in favour of more rather than less regulation; like many with an essentially socialist political outlook, regulation offers them the gains of intervention without any fiscal cost and it is therefore highly tempting. One can be quite unsure how this will play out over a few decades of further EU membership. So far, these problems may have been patched up to a reasonable extent, judging from the indicators we have examined. However, the proclaimed aim of the EU is ever-closer union, effectively a state with a strong top-down central power. Even if pro-EU politicians in the UK have proclaimed repeatedly that we should not take this aim seriously, it has been apparent in practice that it is deadly serious, as the actions to implement it have been rolled out. It follows that, ultimately, the resulting top-down regulative structure that would emerge would consistently violate the UK's traditional free market approach.

GROWTH AND REGULATION

So far, we have examined the one-off permanent costs of regulation on the UK. However, there has been increasing concern over the 'dynamic' effects of such measures; by this is meant the effects on growth. Such dynamic effects implicitly rise over time in that growth is stunted by them. Plainly, such potential costs are therefore extremely serious. However, it has proved difficult to find evidence of causal linkages between regulation or associated business costs due, for example, to taxation and growth. There have been many studies showing that there is a statistical link between the two, but causation cannot be demonstrated by such studies.

In the Appendix we review recent research (Minford, 2015; Minford and Meenagh, 2020) in which evidence of causation has been established. This work represents something of a breakthrough in the long-standing debate over causal evidence in this area. The specific effect of a sustained ten-year 5% rise in the measure of intervention (equivalent to a rise in the effective tax rate) on growth is, as noted there, for a fall in growth of 1.5% a year over two decades. This is a substantial effect, which tends to dwarf the other effects in this book. It means, for example, that if the EU were to raise the implicit tax represented by its regulatory interventions by an average of 1.7% over the next decade, by 2035 the UK would be some 10% poorer; to put this in perspective, our estimate of the tax equivalent imposed to date by the EU is around 6%, imposing a similar 6% of GDP cost on the UK. So, a further rise in the implicit tax of 1.7% would only represent a rise of about a third. Unfortunately, such a rise seems entirely possible given the parameters within which 'ever-closer union' would operate, allowing harmonization of all areas of tax and regulation along the lines of the general continental model; indeed, it could well be a gross underestimate.

CONCLUSIONS

Central to the functioning of any economy is its regulative regime; this acts as a complement to the tax regime in establishing how business friendly and pro-competitive the environment is. A regime that permits cheap entry for new businesses and low ongoing costs of doing business encourages competition and so innovation. Though the 'Single Market' in regulation is often extolled as a model of a 'level playing field' that encourages competition, what is found in surveys of business opinion is that product regulation in the EU is intrusive and may favour large incumbents, while labour market regulation doles out rights for workers that are expensive for employers to honour, discourage employment and deter business expansion. We may also note that business taxation itself varies markedly across EU countries and is not yet 'harmonized'; however, for the UK with its relatively low marginal tax rates on business and high earners, there could also exist a threat under 'ever-closer union' that this too could be jeopardized. Using the Liverpool Model of the UK (Marwaha et al., 1984), with its pioneering treatment of the supply side, we have found that there are high potential costs to the economy from a large-scale extension of EU regulation. On top of these one-off ('static') costs, such an extension also threatens substantial potential 'dynamic' costs (i.e., reductions in the UK's growth rate). The remedy for these threats is a new treaty in which EU product regulations only apply to the sectors exporting to the EU and non-product (e.g., labour) regulations do not apply at all. The UK would then be free to choose its own regulative non-product regime and decide case by case on what product regimes it will adopt for products not exported to the EU.

APPENDIX: EVALUATING MARGARET THATCHER'S REFORMS: BRITAIN'S 1980S ECONOMIC REFORM PROGRAMME

The aims of Margaret Thatcher's reform programme were to cure the 'British disease' of the 1970s: low growth, high inflation and high unemployment. It had two main elements: 'monetarism' (namely, monetary policy and complementary fiscal policy to defeat inflation) and 'supply-side policy'. This last in turn consisted of two main components: labour market flexibility to reduce unemployment and the reduction of barriers to entrepreneurial activity (taxes and regulations) to raise productivity growth. These reforms were deliberately sequenced for practical political reasons (see Minford, 1998 for more details of these policies).

Monetarism and the defeat of inflation came first. Then, starting in her second term, Margaret Thatcher embarked on her supply-side programme, which would then also occupy her third term. A key element that helped her in the supply-side reforms was that, inflation having been defeated, demand policy was reasonably free to support them.

The Monetarist Programme

The programme to defeat inflation, then running at close to 20%, was formulated as a 'gradualist' one, following advice from Milton Friedman (explained in Friedman, 1980). It would reduce both the growth of M3[2] (a proxy for bank credit) and the fiscal deficit as a share of GDP – the latter included (against Friedman's advice) to ensure credibility of the monetary target, as emphasized in rational expectations models.

In the event, 'the best-laid plans *gang aft agley* [go awry]' and both these targets were substantially overshot, as Figures A3.1 and A3.2 show. The recession was the cause of the overshoot in both. The deficit (measured here by the public sector borrowing requirement, PSBR) surged as welfare benefits rose and revenues fell with falling GDP and rising unemployment. Bank credit and so M3, the chosen indicator, grew rapidly as firms hit by falling receipts borrowed heavily from the banks to stay in business; the Bank of England, which was opposed to monetarist policies, lent supportively to the banks to facilitate this.

Faced with these overshoots, the government could have abandoned the policies and accepted defeat. However, instead, Margaret Thatcher pressed on, insisting that the money supply and budget deficits would be curbed to ensure the defeat of inflation, whatever the short-term pain. The main focus was on fiscal policy: the fiscal stance was tightened in the 1981 budget to boost policy credibility. As long-run interest rates came down, it also permitted a cut in interest rates on the grounds that monetary conditions as measured by money supply indicators other than the chosen one were in fact rather too tight – see Figure A3.3 on M4.

As is well known, the critical 1981 budget attracted strong criticism in the famous letter to *The Times* from 364 economists: the mass of UK economists, who generally opposed the policies, preferring price/wage controls and demand stimulus, argued that the policies would create long-running recession, with little if any effect on inflation (Booth, 2006).

However, they were wrong, as Figure A3.6 on inflation shows. By the end of 1982, inflation had fallen below 5%. Furthermore, growth in 1982 picked up sharply, signalling the end of the recession. Unemployment stayed high, but it became plain that this was not through lack of demand, but because of supply-side problems in the labour market: real wages were being held at unrealistically high levels by unconditionally provided unemployment benefits and powerful unions. Also, manufacturing productivity was low after years of subsidies and loose control of credit. It became clear that the supply-side programme must be ushered in.

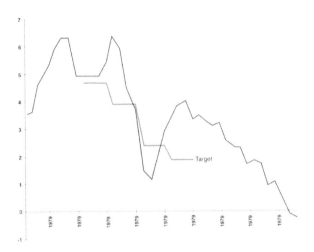

Source: Adapted in simplified form from Minford (1998), Figure 4.5.

Figure A3.1   PSBR/GDP four-quarter average

The Supply-side Reforms, Part One: Labour Market Flexibility

The first part of the programme was focused on labour market flexibility. The unemployment benefits/wage ratio was curbed; eligibility for these benefits was made conditional on proper search, to be monitored in job market interviews at the benefit office under a 'Restart' review. Union strike powers were cut back: strikes would be permitted only after a full members' ballot and only over the pay/conditions of members – no 'secondary action' would be allowed, that is, strikes by other workers at suppliers or customers of the employing firm. Strikes in breach of these laws would not be protected against tort contract violation by existing 'union immunities' (these allowed unions to 'induce contract violation' legally); so civil court action against unions over illegal strikes could and did lead to large-scale damages and fines. These measures proved to be highly

Source: Adapted in simplified form from Minford (1998), Figure 4.6.

Figure A3.2   Annual percentage growth in M3

effective in curbing strikes and lowering incentives to avoid job search –
see Figures A3.4 and A3.5. Figure A3.5 on the benefit/wage ratio relates
to the basic benefit for a low-paid worker where unemployment was
concentrated. In addition, there was an earnings-related supplement for
higher-paid workers; this was abolished in 1982. Strong conditionality on
paying benefits was also introduced in 1986 under the 'Restart' process.
Figure A3.6 shows the effect on inflation of the monetarist policies and
Figure A 3.7 shows both actual unemployment and the estimates from the
Liverpool supply-side model of the UK for the natural/equilibrium unemployment rate emerging from these reforms. It can be seen that by the
end of the 1980s, both actual and equilibrium unemployment had fallen
greatly. Actual unemployment was to rise again sharply at the start of the
1990s as a result of recession associated with UK entry into the European
Exchange Rate Mechanism (ERM) in 1990, a serious policy mistake.
But, otherwise, unemployment has been on a steady downward path to
its latest rate of around 2% on the benefits-claimant measure used here.

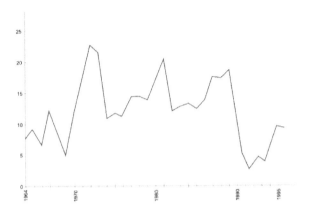

Source: Adapted in simplified form from Minford (1998), Figure 10.

Figure A3.3   M4 growth

The Supply-side Reforms, Part Two: Improved Environment for Entrepreneurs

For entrepreneurial firms seeking to raise productivity, regulative inter-vention in the labour market via union powers and social intervention (labour rights) was a major issue in pre-Thatcher Britain. Hence, the labour market flexibility reforms just examined also constituted an important element in the improvement of the entrepreneurial environ-ment. The other main element involved taxes on entrepreneurs – notably, the top marginal income tax rates and corporate (or corporation) tax on small and medium-sized enterprises (SMEs).

It has proved difficult to find evidence of causal linkages between such business disincentives and productivity growth. There have been many studies showing that there is a statistical link between the two, but causa-tion cannot be demonstrated by such studies (Minford, Meenagh and Wang, 2007). Figures A3.8 and A3.9 on UK manufacturing productivity growth and its comparison with West Germany show the way relative productivity surged in the UK after 1979 as compared with the poor

post-war performance up to 1979. But we need serious causal analysis to
establish a link with the reforms.

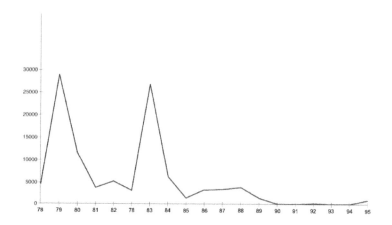

Source: Adapted in simplified form from Minford (1998), Figure 5.2.

Figure A3.4   Working days lost in strikes

In recent research (Minford, 2015; Minford and Meenagh, 2020), evidence of causation has been established. A model of the UK economy
in which regulatory costs affect productivity growth is simulated to
generate behaviour of GDP and productivity, as well as other economic
variables over the period from 1970 to 2009. If this model is a correct
representation of the UK, then the behaviour of the economy we actually
observed in this period should be accounted for by these simulations.
This work finds that one cannot reject this hypothesis statistically with
95% confidence.

First, we may inspect the data on tax and labour market regulation
(LMR) in the UK over this period of the Thatcher reforms. In Panel 1 of
Figure A3.10 are three series: the top marginal income tax rate, the small
company corporate tax rate, and LMR (mainly reflecting union laws). In
Panel 2 are two series representing different weighted combinations of

these, Tau (1) and Tau (2).[3] For the main results, Tau (1), which equally weights LMR and the top marginal rate, is used; however, the results are robust to using Tau (2), which replaces the top marginal rate with the corporate tax rate.

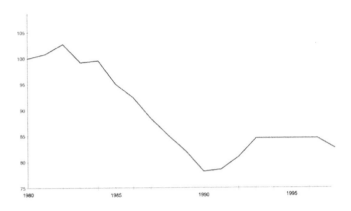

Source: Adapted in simplified form from Minford (1998), Figure 5.3.

Figure A3.5   *Benefits – excluding earning-related supplement – relative to real wages (1980 = 100)*

The method of testing involved here is indirect inference, checking whether the simulated behaviour of the UK economy growth model was the same as its actual behaviour. In this instance, the behaviour is relationships between output, productivity and the tax/regulation variable. It turns out that the hypothesis that the simulated behaviour is the same as the actual behaviour has a p-value of 0.18, well above the 0.05 rejection threshold. Figures A3.11 and A3.12 illustrate how similar the actual behaviour and the average simulated behaviour are for these variables; this underpins the similarity of the actual and the simulated relationships between them.

This work represents something of a breakthrough in the longstanding debate over causal evidence in this area. The specific effect of a sustained ten-year 5% rise in the measure of intervention (equivalent to a rise in the effective tax rate) on growth is for a fall in growth of 1.5% a year over two decades – about 30% in total. Over the 1980s, the intervention measure (Tau in Figure A3.10) fell between 5 and 20%, depending on which measure one uses: the effect on the growth rate of productivity could therefore have been between 1.5 and 6%. This is a substantial effect.

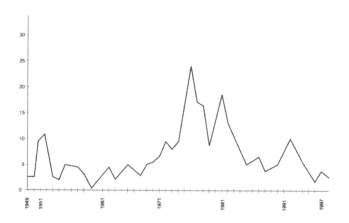

Source: Adapted in simplified form from Minford (1998), Figure 4.3.

Figure A3.6   Retail Price Index (RPI) inflation – all items.

A Note on the Political Economy of Margaret Thatcher's Reforms

One of the apparent puzzles of the Thatcher reforms is how they came to be politically possible, given the large-scale forces arrayed against them. For a start, big business, as typified by the Confederation of British Industry, was against monetarism with its elimination of easy credit and the end of the associated devaluations. It was also against union reform, since unions acted as an effective entry barrier to new, especially SME, firms. Meanwhile, of course, unions and the political left were against the reduction in wage inflation and the curbing of union powers. The

Conservative Party was split, with 'one-nation Tories' opposed to the reforms on all these grounds. This created a constant fear of leadership challenge within the Thatcher government. In response to this threat, Margaret Thatcher put key economic portfolios in the hands of trusted allies – Howe, Lawson, Ridley and Tebbit. Her opponents, lacking economics expertise, found it hard to challenge this group on economic grounds.

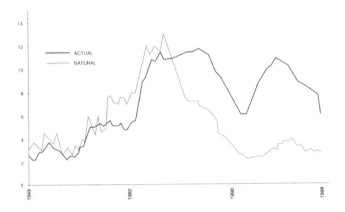

Source: Adapted in simplified form from Minford (1998), Figure 5.5.

Figure A3.7   Actual and natural rates of unemployment

The main support for Margaret Thatcher came from the skilled working class, whose interests manual unions undermined by pushing up manual wages and disrupting production at the expense of profits and so skilled wages. Adding to this support, the defeat of inflation was extremely popular: inflation, with its effects in redistributing resources to those lucky or smart enough to do well from inflation, had become highly unpopular. The other central policy of 'bringing unions within the law' was also widely acclaimed.

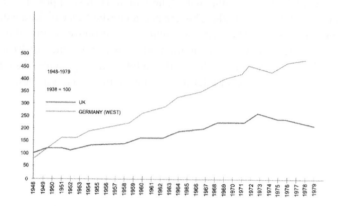

Source: Adapted in simplified form from Minford (1998), Figure 3.9.

Figure A3.8   *Manufacturing productivity in Germany and the UK*
1948–79

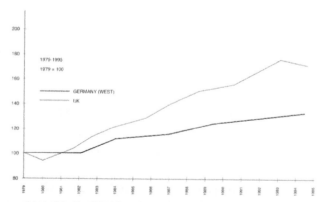

Source: Adapted in simplified form from Minford (1998), Figure 3.9.

Figure A3.9   *Manufacturing productivity in Germany and the UK*
1979–95

However, the key element that buttressed Margaret Thatcher's position
was Conservative Party compromise, faced with the threat of a far

left-wing Labour government under Michael Foot (a close parallel with the 2019 threat of a Corbyn government). Hence, the secret of the reforms' feasibility and success was the willingness of the Conservative Party to maintain its power, to back the reform programme and combine with its 'new working class' support base. One of the main intermediaries between the Conservative one-nation group and Margaret Thatcher was William, later made Lord, Whitelaw, who explained these realities to his old-guard friends. In recording her gratitude to him for his efforts and loyalty in buttressing her governments, Margaret Thatcher much later remarked that 'Everyone needs a Willie'. Needless to say, in spite of the ensuing hilarity, it was not a joke, and indeed jokes were not her style – rather, she made remarks that were barbed with wit, as when after a dinner celebrating the Institute of Economic Affairs' 50th anniversary in 2005 when speaking last after a long line-up of men she remarked slightly testily that 'The cock may crow but it's the hen that lays the eggs'.

Conclusions

The reform programme of the Thatcher governments is widely regarded as a success story in curing the 1970s' ailments – inflation, slow growth and rising unemployment – of the British economy, then 'the sick man of Europe'. They began with UK monetarism, and followed with labour market reforms, and finally with the reshaping of taxes and government spending to help the rebirth of an entrepreneurial economy. The early monetarist phase was meant to be gradualist, but mistakes delivered a very sharp squeeze; as people understood that the policy regime had changed, inflation fell quickly and growth recovered. The labour market reforms brought down unemployment by raising work incentives; aided by falling tax rates the environment became propitious for entrepreneurs, raising productivity growth. Margaret Thatcher was able to assemble the support for this ambitious agenda to succeed politically against many opposing interests because of the ability of the Conservative Party to unite its traditional middle-class constituency with the newly emerging, aspiring skilled working-class constituency that had a strong interest in these reforms.

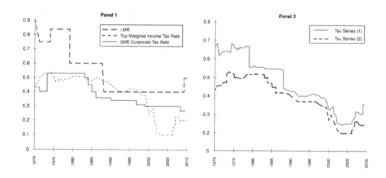

Source: Minford and Meenagh (2020), Figure 2.

*Figure A3.10   Data on tax and labour market regulation (LMR) in the
            UK during the Thatcher reforms*

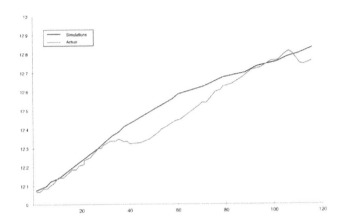

Source: Minford and Meenagh (2020).

Figure A3.11   Match of average simulated and actual output

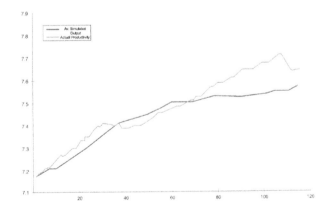

Source: Minford and Meenagh (2020).

Figure A3.12   Match of average simulated output to actual productivity

NOTES

1. This chapter partially draws on material in Chapter 2 of Minford et al. (2015).
2. These M numbers are various definitions of the money supply, starting from the narrowest M0 (notes, coin and bank reserves at Bank of England), M1 (M0 + bank current account deposits), M2 (M1+ time deposits), M3 (M2 and large time deposits, institutional money market funds, short-term repurchase agreements and larger liquid assets), up to M4 (M3 + all time and savings deposits).
3. Tau is the authors' measure of tax and regulation burden on entrepreneurs; there are two alternatives.

REFERENCES

Beecroft, A. (2012), *Report on Employment Law* [the Beecroft Report], London: Department for Business, Innovation & Skills, accessed 27 August 2020 at www.gov.uk/government/publications/employment-law-review-report-beecroft.

Booth, P. (ed.) (2006), *Were 364 Economists All Wrong?*, London: Institute of Economic Affairs.

Congdon, T. (2014), *The City of London in Retreat: The EU's Attack on Britain's Most Successful Industry*, London: The Bruges Group.

Friedman, M. (1980), 'Response to questionnaire on monetary policy', in *The House of Commons Treasury and Civil Service Committee*: *Memorandum on Monetary Policy*. *Great Britain, Parliamentary Papers (Commons), Session 1979–1980, 720, part 1 (July 1980)*, pp. 1–4, 55–61. London: Her Majesty's Stationery Office.

Gwartney, J., R. Lawson and J. Hall (eds) (2012), *Economic Freedom of the World, 2012 Annual Report*, Vancouver: Fraser Institute.

Marwaha, S., K. Matthews, P. Minford and A. Sprague (1984), 'The Liverpool macroeconomic model of the United Kingdom', *Economic Modelling*, **1** (1), 24–62.

Minford, L. (2015), 'The impact of policy on UK output and productivity growth, 1970–2009: testing an open economy DSGE model', PhD thesis, Cardiff University.

Minford, L. and D. Meenagh (2020), 'Supply-side policy and economic growth: a case study of the UK', *Open Economies Review*, **31** (1), 159–93.

Minford, P. (1998), *Markets Not Stakes: The Triumph of Capitalism and the Stakeholder Fallacy*, London: Orion Business Books.

Minford, P., with S. Gupta, V.P.M. Le, V. Mahambare and Y. Xu (2015), *Should Britain Leave the EU? An Economic Analysis of a Troubled Relationship*, 2nd edition, Cheltenham, UK and Northampton, MA, USA: Edward Elgar Publishing.

Minford, P., D. Meenagh and Ji. Wang (2007), 'Growth and relative living standards – testing barriers to riches on post-war panel data', *Cardiff Economics Working Papers*, No. E2007/12, Cardiff University.

4. An agenda for tax reform

INTRODUCTION

Forty years ago, Margaret Thatcher inaugurated nearly two decades of reform, designed to restore Britain economically to the low inflation and dynamic economy it had once been. In 1997, when the New Labour government obtained power, its leaders proclaimed that it would use the free market to pursue efficiency while also striving for 'social justice'. In a number of areas that was achieved. In monetary policy, the Bank of England was made independent; in fiscal policy, the government announced various new rules to buttress fiscal responsibility, though it then went on to spend heavily and irresponsibly; in the labour market, the tough approach to benefit eligibility inaugurated by the Conservatives was made bipartisan. Thus, some progress was made.

However, in other crucial areas, no progress was made; indeed, we have slipped back. In no area is this more evident than in taxation and benefits (renamed 'tax credits'). Complexity has proliferated, with a stress on special incentives and special penalties. This has created a complex patchwork of high marginal tax rates. This, and how to reform it, is the topic of this chapter.

WHAT IS A GOOD TAX SYSTEM? THE RAMSEY PRINCIPLE

It is useful to recap on just what, from the viewpoint of economic efficiency, is the best tax system. The key principle is due to Ramsey[1] and is known as the Ramsey Principle of equalizing tax across groups, commodities and time.

The basic idea is that as the tax rate increases, the extra cost becomes steadily higher (call it the law of increasing dysfunction). The formal reason is that the state is driving a bigger and bigger wedge between what things (e.g., labour) are worth in the market and the (net-of-tax) return to the people producing them; the latter is the true cost of the effort being expended, the former is the true value to the economy. So, as taxes increase and output falls, the loss of that output is increasingly damaging because the loss of value to the economy is ever greater, while the reduction in effort gained is ever smaller.

On the other hand, where the tax rate falls and output increases, the gain from that higher output gets steadily smaller because the extra value is getting closer and closer to the extra cost. The corollary of this principle is that when the output responsiveness is the same across different markets (a natural benchmark), tax rates should be equalized because at this point there is no gain from switching the tax burden from one commodity to another, as the extra gain on one would be just equal to the extra loss on the other. The three practical implications are that:

- the celebrated 'tax neutrality' (across goods and different activities, methods of finance etc.) principle of the Lawson years should be reintroduced;
- the tax system should move towards a flat rate tax (the same rate across all groups of people regardless of their earnings); and
- the less well-known idea of 'tax smoothing', which is keeping the tax rate for the economy constant over time, should be the foundation for public borrowing policy.

NEUTRALITY ACROSS SECTORS AND ACTIVITIES

Under Nigel Lawson's chancellorship, a determined effort was made to achieve neutrality so that different activities should attract the same marginal tax rate as far as possible. Capital allowances were reduced so that they reflected economic depreciation rates; stamp duty was largely abolished, as were preferential rates of tax for privileged activities such as 'development zones'.

Gordon Brown reversed this thrust in a bout of unprecedented activism, and this activism continued under the Treasury tenure of George Osborne. We now have capital allowances back again, to 'encourage investment'. Stamp duty on houses (a tax on mobility) has been raised sharply, with a top rate of 13%. Tax privilege is back for 'derelict zones'. There are special low rates of tax, both income and capital gains, for small and medium-sized enterprises (SMEs) on the grounds that their activity is particularly fruitful. Saving in various forms has been penalized, notably by the abolition of Advance Corporation Tax (ACT) relief for pension funds but also by the sharp raising of the level of the old-age benefit threshold (now called a minimum) and by the introduction of pension tax credits for those with pension incomes above this threshold.

Previously, the philosophy had been to relieve saving of income tax in most approved (long-term) forms, thus moving income tax in the direction of a tax on consumption – again in line with the Ramsey Principle – in that future consumption is thereby taxed at the same rate as current consumption. The aim of reform should be to get rid of special treatment. The concept that should underlie the taxation of commodities and services should be that of taxing consumption, however it is carried out, at a standard percentage rate. In principle, value-added tax (VAT) should be extended as far as possible across all categories of spending, so making possible a reduction in its standard rate. At the same time, income tax should be adjusted onto a consumption tax basis: this would mean that all saving would be deducted from income before it is taxed. This would abolish the mass of saving exemptions, as they would now be redundant. It would also simplify the system. Since these exemptions have much the same value as the total relief of savings via the consumption tax, there is little if any extra cost involved. The consumption tax base would enable the abolition of capital gains tax, which is most unsatisfactory in principle (because it taxes saving) and also complicated in application. Consumption is then calculated as:

Income (including capital gains) – the difference between end-period and beginning-period asset values

Since the change in asset values includes capital gains, this tax base amounts to:

Income (excluding capital gains) – any net new asset acquisition

The simplification, incidentally, of tax returns would be huge: instead of the present mass of detail, it would be just income less any net new assets.

One may note in passing that stamp duty, which is a tax on transactions, not on any consumption value, should be abolished. The same applies to a number of recently introduced taxes such as airport tax and insurance tax. Only if such taxes are related directly to charges for services rendered do they have a justification; in this case, it would be better for them to be levied explicitly as charges and then passed on to the customer in whatever way the commercial operators feel is best. Airport charges, for example, should be levied on airport operators.

Another important point to note is that the consumption tax is levied on all consumption; this includes consumption of all housing that is a long-lived consumer asset. Rented housing is taxed automatically with a consumption tax. However, under a consumption tax, saving to buy a house is untaxed; under an income tax, house purchases are paid for out of taxed income. It follows that the consumption of owner-occupied housing would be taxed under a consumption tax in the same way that rent is taxed. In switching to a consumption tax, this implies that no more tax is paid on owner-occupied housing than it is now; it is merely taxed in a different way.

In what follows, I assume that the rates above the ordinary top rate are abolished, as in our Brexit Fund proposals set out in Chapter 7. I focus entirely on replacing existing income tax rates (including the 'super-rates above 40%) by a flat consumption tax.

THE FLAT RATE TAX

Table 4.1 shows that the UK tax system (income tax, National Insurance [NI] and indirect tax included) produces a top marginal tax rate of about 60%. This is the percentage of the wage paid by an employer taken by the state in NI, indirect tax and income tax.

Table 4.1   Calculation of the top marginal tax rate on £100 gross earnings

Higher-rate Taxpayer	
Total employer costs (inc. NI)	£113.80
Employee gross earnings	£100.00
Employee net earnings (after income tax and employee NI)	£58.00
Indirect tax (VAT & net excise duties @ 21.8%)	£10.40
Cost of goods	£47.60
Marginal tax rate	58.2%

Note: VAT and net excise duties estimated at 21.8% (adjustment to factor cost/ consumption at factor cost). Figures rounded to the nearest 10 pence.
Source: Author's calculations.

It is calculated by estimating what the total wage cost paid by an employer for an employee buys for that employee in terms of actual consumption enjoyed, as a percentage of the wage cost. It turns out that higher-paid employees get approximately £48 worth of goods and services valued at their true cost for an extra £114 paid for their labour by their employer – a marginal tax rate of 58%. For the employee on average earnings, the equivalent marginal tax rate is about 48%.

The average tax rate of the economy is 40%. In this, the average yield of income tax is about 20% – this is the result of an average of bands from 10% to 40%. So, a flat rate tax of the same yield, assuming none of the indirect effects on revenue discussed later, would be, allowing for the personal tax threshold, some 25% against the current mixture. (All figures in this discussion are inevitably approximate given the complexity of the tax system.)

Under the flat rate principle, personal allowances are unjustifiable because they imply a rise in the necessary flat rate tax – in effect, personal allowances can be thought of as a zero-tax band for people on very low earnings, which violates the flat rate optimum. Abolishing personal allowances would increase the tax base by about another fifth, allowing the flat rate to drop to 20% for the same yield.

We will consider later the possible ways in which the flat rate might be introduced in practice; in its basic form, it poses a number of practical difficulties. Yet, its essential gains can be obtained quite simply. But first we consider the question of benefits (negative tax or tax credits).

THE BENEFITS SYSTEM

Benefits have now largely been renamed tax credits and are administered by HM Revenue & Customs (HMRC). The problem with the current tax credit system is the very high marginal tax rates created by their means testing – currently the withdrawal rate is 37%, which added to other taxes and NI implies a marginal rate of around 70%.

These benefits have various purposes. Family tax credit is intended to increase work income relative to unemployment benefit, so as to make work worthwhile. It is also designed to help poor people with children, in order to reduce the poverty of families. Housing benefit is intended to help poor people pay for housing with rents set by market forces; thus, the idea is to shift subsidies from bricks and mortar (council housing), which stops people moving to find jobs, directly to the people intended to be helped. Finally, other classes of benefit are explicitly designed to help with particular situations, such as disability; provided these benefits are dependent on these situations and not on income they do not create disincentives to acquire income by work. The major class is pensions (see

Minford, 2005). Here my focus is only on benefits that primarily affect work incentives.

In themselves, these purposes are worthy. The problem is that, on the one hand, they are expensive in taxes – which drags down the welfare and efficiency of the general taxpayer; and, on the other hand, they create serious disincentives (via those high marginal tax rates) for the very people they are helping to work and retrain. Hence, it is important to try to find ways of reducing both their tax cost and their disincentives for the recipients.

One way of reducing the tax burden is to lower tax credits to the 'poverty threshold'; this is entirely reasonable, given that their objective is to relieve poverty. Unemployment income is designed so that its recipients reach socially acceptable minimum levels of consumption. Therefore, by implication, this is also the level that tax credits should achieve as a minimum for families with working heads; they are, in fact, significantly higher, in the order of 10%. The reason given for their being higher is that it provides a monetary incentive to work.

However, this makes no sense. The premiss of unemployment support is that it is only to be paid to those who cannot yet find a job; after a period of search they are meant to take a job and then this support is withdrawn. This conditionality ('no fifth option' in Blairite Labour par-lance; in Conservative terms, the Jobseeker's Allowance) is now being enforced in a bipartisan manner, as it is generally accepted that people should take available jobs rather than stay on benefits for extended periods. If so, the monetary incentive is irrelevant, as, once the time is up, the unemployment support is withdrawn. Thus, we can easily justify this minimum or meanness in the provision of welfare benefits to those in work by the argument that in fact it creates no disincentive to work when benefits are administered toughly so that work must be taken.

A further way of reducing the cost to the taxpayer is to means-test the tax credits for people in work more sharply – that is, to withdraw them more quickly as income rises. The age-old problem this causes is that the poor then face a worse poverty trap since the incentive to retrain for better-paid work is apparently very small. But, in fact, one can argue with some plausibility that it is best to have a short range of income over which the withdrawal rate is very high (for some earlier calculations, see Minford, 1990). The idea of this is that while incentives in this range are very poor, the range is nevertheless small enough that the most serious retraining would allow trainees to 'leap over' it, in the sense that their income after training would be well above the range and hence the marginal tax rate would be moderate across the leap. Under these circumstances, the poverty trap would not cause very much damage to retraining plans but would bring the cost of family and related credits down considerably for the taxpayer. The latter cost element in the calculation arises from the shape of the working population distribution: as support is extended up the income range, the number of people involved rises disproportionately.

A further principle originally enunciated by Sir Norman Fowler in his review of benefits in the mid-1980s – that the state should only support families with children – is now adopted by the main parties. The idea is that single people can help themselves, as can childless couples, since both can work. Thus, the concept of poverty as the concern of the state essentially relates to families with children. By eliminating a large class of recipients, this again validly avoids both the cost to the taxpayer and the disincentives to those assisted.

With the aid of this analysis, recent moves on tax credits can be seen to have been misguided. The withdrawal range for them has been stretched virtually up to average earnings. Also, in order (mistakenly as we have seen) to create an 'incentive to work' they have been raised in amount to some 10% or so above unemployment support levels. Our principles suggest that the support should be cut back to the unemployment level and that withdrawal rates should be fast, as they were before 1997.

Housing benefit is in essence, or should be, another credit. It can be treated similarly. Currently, it is paid to benefit recipients in respect of their actual housing bills, hence creating no incentive to economize on housing. It would be better instead to pay them an amount to the value necessary to reach the same level of housing. This should be withdrawn as above – fast. Families will then all shop around for housing just like ordinary unsupported families do today.

It is clear that, until the 1997 Labour government lowered the withdrawal rate, similar calculations informed Treasury thinking for many years.

'TAX SMOOTHING'

Tax smoothing is the principle that the tax rate should be set at the constant level that would pay the government's expected bills into the indefinite future. What would this constant tax rate be? It turns out that it would be a rate sufficient to pay for average government spending as a proportion of gross domestic product (GDP) and also to keep government debt from rising as a proportion of GDP. This last implies that taxes must cover debt interest adjusted for inflation and also less an allowance for growth (because growth reduces debt as a proportion of GDP).

To illustrate the idea of tax smoothing in a practical way, consider what will happen under this formula if there is some unexpected shock – say a recession or a public spending crisis (a war perhaps) – which raises spending or lowers the yield of taxation. Then the implication is that the tax rate should only change by the implied permanent worsening of the finances. What is this? Suppose taxes fall by £20 billion for a year but are expected to recover completely. Then debt will rise by this amount: interest costs adjusted for growth will rise by £20 billion times the real interest rate minus the growth rate. The following calculation shows that the flat tax rate should be increased so that it yields an additional £0.1 billion. Assuming that the real interest rate is 3%, and the growth rate is 2.5%:

$$£20 \ billion \times (3\% - 2.5\%) = £20 \ billion \times 0.5\% = £0.1 \ billion$$

The implication of tax smoothing is that public debt fluctuations are used to 'smooth tax rates' – and that it should not be an objective of policy to pay off debt for its own sake (indeed, public debt is necessary for the proper working of the private savings and pension markets). In practice, one may want to qualify the tax-smoothing principle a bit over the business cycle – for demand or supply reasons – but as a basic benchmark for long periods of time in considering where one should be pushing tax rates, it is highly robust.

Another practical implication of tax smoothing is that the relevant cost of public spending is the whole future stream of spending not just the amount being spent today. Hence, for example, if reform to public services were instituted with the effect of causing economies over a fairly long period of time, then these economies can be counted today in setting tax rates. Of course, delayed economies in this do not count as much as immediate economies because one has to pay interest on the debt created by the delay, but they do count to some extent. What this means is that borrowing can rise to take the strain of lower taxes until the benefits of spending reforms work through.

This tax-smoothing principle is therefore the key to making tax and other public sector reforms feasible because it enjoins us to take account of the long-run effects of reform on growth and tax revenue. Borrowing should be used to fill the gaps between revenue and spending that occur en route, with the tax rate set in the long run to balance the budget in steady state.

THE 'SCOPE' FOR TAX CUTS: THE LAFFER CURVE AND GROWTH EFFECTS

Hence, an important implication of the tax-smoothing formula is for the extent of tax cuts that can be afforded. Since the formula looks forward to the full path of foreseeable spending and tax revenues, plainly the effects of any policy change on that whole future path is of vital importance to the calculation. It makes no sense to exclude from it anything other than the current situation minus the obvious 'direct' effects of the tax cut, as has traditionally been done in tax reform calculations.

Since the Reagan and Thatcher periods in the US and the UK, a mass of work has been done on the effects of tax cuts. The consensus has changed within the economics profession: there is now a cautious acceptance that tax cuts have significant effects both on net revenues in the short to medium term and on the growth rate of the economy. The first of these is the 'Laffer effects'.[2] These stipulate fairly rapid (i.e., within two to four years) effects on the supply of work, effort and tax avoidance of lower marginal tax rates. These effects create a 'net revenue recovery' or 'back flow', partially offsetting the loss of revenue from cutting tax rates. For example, a study for the UK found that the response to the top tax rate of higher earners' labour supply was approximately 1% for a 1% cut in the top marginal rate (see Minford and Ashton, 1991). Using this response, it was possible to replicate the effect on tax revenues of Nigel Lawson's cut in the top rate from 60% to 40%. Further down the income distribution, the proportional response fell: the average response was about half of 1%. That would imply that cutting the top overall marginal tax rate by 10% today would cause a net loss of revenue of only half the 'direct' amount.

The second set of effects, on growth, are potentially more important still. These have come into focus from research in the past decade into 'endogenous growth' (i.e., the study of how government policy on spending and taxation can affect growth). A large number of empirical studies have found an effect of tax rates on growth. Empirical evidence alone might be questioned on the grounds that other mechanisms might have raised growth and reduced taxes. However, economic theory too has made progress in identifying the causes at work. One is an interaction with the effect of lower tax rates in stimulating labour supply: higher employment promotes 'learning by doing' (the more people work, the more they learn). This extra rate of knowledge acquisition raises productivity growth.

Another effect is on risk-taking and entrepreneurship: lower taxes mean that individuals and firms will take more risks to get extra income, which will mean more innovation and so higher productivity growth at the level of the economy (at this level, individual risks cancel out, rather like competition that causes individuals to lose out to others while benefiting society as a whole).

If we turn to the quantities involved, the typical response found in empirical studies is for the growth rate to rise by one-third of the proportional cut in marginal tax rates (for a survey and discussion of these results, see Minford and Wang, 2011, and for more recent results in a full causal analysis, see Minford and Meenagh, 2020). For example, if the marginal tax rate fell by 10% on average across the economy (from 40% to 36% say), then the growth rate would rise by 3.3% (from 2.5% to 2.58% p.a. say). While these studies do not establish causality, more recent work on the Thatcher tax/regulation reforms tests for and finds causality, as set out in work cited in Chapter 3 (Minford and Meenagh, 2020). It also finds similar orders of magnitude for the effects. These may not sound much, but, of course, they are compounded from year to year, steadily raising revenue.

Alternatively, one may look at it from the viewpoint of spending: if government spending programmes are kept the same as before, this higher growth implies that they will fall steadily as a fraction of GDP, thus enabling tax rates to fall. The exact amount can be found from our formula. It turns out that the permissible new tax rate can fall by a substantial fraction.

To illustrate the formula numerically, take the case where the average marginal tax rate is cut by 10% so that the growth rate rises to 2.58% p.a. The average tax rate as a proportion of GDP can now fall by 6% of GDP, which is no less than £120 billion per year. One can think of this as the permissible initial deficit after the tax cut; by implication, this will be whittled away by growth until eventually the higher revenues would be sufficient to keep the debt/GDP ratio steady again. Now, of course, one would certainly wish to be much more cautious than this.

But the point remains that there is substantial scope to run deficits prudently in the context of cuts in marginal tax rates. One of the main worries of those who have discussed a flat tax is that it would require raising taxes on those on lower than average incomes, in order to keep the direct tax yield constant. However, there is no need for this under our perspective here. In effect, all the key benefits of flatness can be introduced simply by cutting the top income tax rate down to the desired flat rate and leaving the lower rates (including the tax credits as reformed above) alone (for a survey and discussion of these results, see Minford and Wang, 2011, and for more recent results in a full causal analysis, see Minford and Meenagh, 2020). Much of the lost tax revenue would be recouped quickly via the Laffer effect; the rest would be financed by borrowing against the higher growth effects.

TAXES OTHER THAN INCOME

Suppose one accepts the flat rate consumption tax in principle. What should be done about taxes other than income taxes? National Insurance? VAT, customs and excise? Capital gains tax? Inheritance? Corporation tax? Miscellaneous taxes like stamp duty? Let us consider these in turn.

National Insurance (NI) is not in its entirety a tax but a payment in return for an entitlement – namely, the second supplementary pension and insured unemployment benefit. Furthermore, one may 'contract out' of part of it in respect of this second pension. It is, nevertheless, in essence, a tax since it is a compulsory payment in exchange for general government spending. Notice, however, that it is close to a flat rate on 'earned income'. There is a ceiling on the amount of contributions the employee pays but none on what the employer pays. There are thresholds to both. Applying the flat rate principle (but keeping thresholds) means that the employee rate should be uncapped. NI would not be 'rolled into income/consumption tax' because it is paid only by the non-retired as a contribution to pensions (which may be contracted out, a principle that should be retained).

VAT, customs and excise are all consumption taxes. Excise taxes are large imposts on items in highly 'inelastic demand' (i.e., where higher prices cause little reduction in demand); as such, they do not violate the Ramsey Principle because this refers to items with the same general elasticity of response. In fact, it makes sense to levy taxes on inelastic items because they yield extra revenue without altering people's spend-ing patterns much, which is what causes economic costs. As for VAT, it is not all inclusive at the same rate it ought to be to match up to the flat consumption tax principle. It would be best if it could be extended and the rate levelled. However, it is not that far from matching up.

Capital gains tax is part of the income tax that would essentially dis-appear on moving it to a consumption basis. Only if capital gains were partly spent would they be taxed. Inheritance taxes would go. Only if inherited wealth were spent would it be taxed just like other consumption. The reason is simple: the fact that wealth is inherited makes no difference to the point that taxing it implies overtaxing consumption of it, just as the taxation of income on savings does. Taxing assets on the accident of death is in some ways an even worse tax than taxing the income of savings because it is unpredictable. Uncertainty can be a severe disincentive to investment and enterprise.

Corporation tax was, before the abolition of ACT, a rough approximation to an 'imputed tax' on dividends. This meant that when profits were distributed to shareholders, any corporation tax paid on them that year was returned to those shareholders. The main exception was foreign shareholders whose treatment varied with double tax agreements. Since the abolition of ACT, corporation tax has simply become a tax on company profits, with foreign companies being able to claim back certain amounts via double tax agreements. Because of these agreements, this tax has become a lawyers' paradise. However, the tax itself is economically damaging because it penalizes the return on capital. Because capital is free to flow nowadays across borders without exchange controls, this in practice means that it has to recover this cost from consumers, and so it is passed on in prices. But the relative cost of capital and labour is distorted by the tax, creating a wasteful incentive for firms to use less capital and more labour. So, corporation tax can be thought of as similar to an inefficient sales tax.

Lawyers mesmerized by the sums they get back for companies via double tax agreements from foreign Treasuries argue that corporation tax should be kept so that the Treasury can obtain corporation revenues from those foreign Treasuries instead of their clients paying. This is a doubtful argument. True, eliminating corporation tax would eliminate these receipts from foreign Treasuries, but it would also stimulate activity by withdrawing a distorting tax. One way forward would be to keep the tax as one paid by corporations and thus eligible for double tax agreements, but to levy it as a value-added tax that would retain its revenue qua consumption levy while eliminating its distortionary impact.

Finally, miscellaneous taxes like stamp duty and airline tax should be treated as taxes on transactions. These are, in general, poor taxes since they do not correspond to consumption values. If they caused no change in behaviour patterns, they could be justified on the same basis as excise duties. If they corresponded to economic costs (as with the environment), that could be another justification. However, in the absence of these, they should be converted into consumption-based taxes – for example, to tax housing consumption, the imputed rent value of housing could be incorporated into VAT in place of stamp duty.

What we have seen in this review of the tax system is that existing taxes can be made to conform with the flat rate consumption principle with some modest 'tweaking'. We have also noted that some could be left alone without much damage to the flat rate principle. It is nonsense to think about tax reform as if every change must be balanced in its direct tax effects by other changes. This nonsense that has governed recent government thinking might unkindly be termed 'Micawberist myopia'. It is a needless concession to the enemies of reform because it makes reform almost impossible in practice. Application of the tax-smoothing principle explained above, in conjunction with allowance for Laffer and growth effects, would allow wide-ranging tax reform to be both practicable and responsible.

PRACTICAL STEPS

The application of the flat rate consumption principle can be achieved by a process of successive approximation. Existing taxes can be tweaked or left alone. The main effort can be directed to reforming income tax. Probably the most important element in the flat rate tax is the shift to a consumption base that includes the elimination of capital gains and inheritance taxes, and the inclusion of imputed consumption of owner-occupied housing. The second most important concerns the abolition of the top rate; this could at once be cut from 40% to 22%. Equally important is the reform of tax credits; the main impact on the incentives of poor people comes not from taxation but from benefits discussed above.

I now turn to some rough costings of these changes to the Treasury. There will plainly be an immediate loss of revenue from the cut in the top rates from 40% and 45% at the very top to the standard rate of 20%. According to the standard HMRC 2020 tax ready-reckoner, the cost of this would be £30 billion, about 1.4% of GDP. However, there would be large offsetting gains in revenue from bringing imputed owner-occupied housing into the tax base. In addition, the Laffer effects discussed earlier are likely to recover much of the lost income tax revenue: top rate taxpayers have the highest elasticity. Furthermore, to calculate the growth effect, this cut in the top marginal tax rate of about a half would reduce the top marginal rate from overall taxation by about a third. The permitted fall in revenue due to the growth effect would therefore very easily cover even the direct loss of revenue as discussed earlier. The sticking point for discussions of tax reform has invariably been: how can we pay for it without upsetting numerous people? However, as this discussion reveals, it turns out to be far less problematic than is usually made out. Table 4.2 sets out the key changes and their costs in revenue.

Table 4.2   Key changes in revenue (2020 prices)

Switching to a Consumption Tax Base	£ (billions)
Reduce all income/consumption tax rate (i.e., abolish top rates) to 20%	−30
Abolition of capital gains tax, inheritance tax, stamp duty	−31
Tax at 20% on 6% yield from owner-occupied housing (0.20 × 0.06 × £4700 billion, home-owned housing value)	+56
Subtotal	−5
Further cut in standard (consumption) tax rate (by 5%) to 15%	−42
Growth effect: fall in top marginal tax rate by 23% boosts growth: (10% rise in GDP by 2025, × tax yield of 0.15)	+36
Total	−11 (0.4% of GDP)

Note: Finance this small revenue loss by borrowing against future further growth effects from lower marginal tax rate.
Source: Author calculations, based on HMRC tax ready-reckoner, 2020 prices; Office for Budget Responsibility (OBR) figures for existing revenues; estimates of growth effects from Chapter 3.

It should be noted that these tax reforms would bring the standard (and now flat) income tax rate down to 15% and falling, and would be extremely popular in all social groups. They would be paid for effectively by the rise in employment rates and in growth. With a 15% flat tax, the overall marginal tax rate would drop to 35%. In the longer term, the additional growth would permit the flat tax to fall to 8%, implying an overall marginal rate of 28%.

In politics there is a well-respected principle: for any reform to succeed, there should as few losers as possible. The overall cut in taxation proposed here implies an absence of any major class of losers – the vast majority of those who lose from paying tax on owner-occupied housing or from the uncapping of the employee NI rate will benefit more from the cuts in tax rates. However, inevitably, there will be some individuals for whom there is a serious loss, notably anyone (probably retired) who has a valuable house (bought out of taxed income) but with a small current income. To avoid injustice to these people, an indefinite transitional provision is proposed whereby anyone who would pay more tax under the new system may opt to be taxed under the old system. Since there will be few such people, and since this option will only be available at the time of the crossover, no explicit provision is made for the small cost involved. A precedent lies in the 1998 reform of the housing market when existing tenants were given exemption until they vacated, for their lifetime.

CONCLUSIONS

In this chapter, I have looked at the scope to reform UK taxes. The ideas I have set out are based on old principles that tax should be neutral across commodities and time and should create as little damage to supply incentives as possible. These principles point to reducing marginal tax rates widely through the tax structure, pushing them as close as possible to a flat rate tax system on consumption. Because consumption is a wider tax base than the current income tax base, these reforms would largely pay for themselves. In addition, they would increase growth, bringing in additional revenue, which would allow the flat rate to be put quite low; government borrowing, making use of the tax-smoothing principle, would enable these tax cuts to the flat rate to be brought forward in time. There was a moment at the start of George Osborne's time as chancellor when the government showed interest in these ideas for bringing in a flat tax system. Sadly, the moment passed, and nothing was done. But with the urgent need to maximize Britain's competitiveness as we leave the EU and find a new economic place in the world, this will be a good time to put these ideas into practice.

NOTES

1. Ramsey was a brilliant student at Cambridge in the 1920s and this chapter is based on his 1927 article: 'A contribution to the theory of taxation' in *The Economic Journal*.
2. After Professor Arthur Laffer, their proponent to the Reagan administration, while at Chicago University.

REFERENCES

Minford, P. (1990), 'The poverty trap after the Fowler reforms', in A. Bowen and K. Mayhew (eds), *Improving Incentives for the Low-Paid*, Basingstoke: Palgrave Macmillan, pp. 121–38.

Minford, P. (2005), 'Agenda for a reforming government', *Quarterly Economic Bulletin*, **26** (3), 19–24.

Minford, P. and Ashton (1991), 'The poverty trap and the Laffer curve – what can the GHS tell us?', *Oxford Economic Papers*, **43**, 134–79.

Minford, L. and D. Meenagh (2020), 'Supply-side policy and economic growth: a case study of the UK', *Open Economies Review*, **31** (1), 159–93.

Minford, P. and J. Wang (2011), 'Public spending, taxation and economic growth: the evidence', in P. Booth (ed.), *Sharper Axes, Lower Taxes: Big Steps to a Smaller State*, London: Institute of Economic Affairs, pp. 31–44.

Ramsey, F.P. (1927), 'A contribution to the theory of taxation', *The Economic Journal*, **37** (145), 47–61.

PART II

Supporting Britain's economy through fiscal and monetary policy

5. Fiscal and monetary policy for the post-Brexit world

In this chapter, I discuss what the UK's current economic situation demands in the way of fiscal and monetary policy responses. We must begin from the widespread dissatisfaction the public expresses about current policy, not least with the persistence of 'austerity' policies since the financial crisis. This dissatisfaction has led to demands by some for a return to socialist policies and an abandonment of 'capitalism'; this was the political position of Jeremy Corbyn's Labour Party. We have seen similar positions being taken, rather surprisingly, even in the US Democratic Party, which traditionally supported the general capitalist economic model. So, what is this opposition to capitalism all about?

THE PROBLEMS OF CAPITALISM AND HOW TO FIX THEM

When the people rage against the dominant system, as has been occurring across the West in recent years, with 'populist' insurrections one after the other, we should sit up and take notice, with proposals to avoid such things in future.

Several books have been written recently (Niemietz, 2019; Zitelmann, 2018) explaining well how dreadful 'socialism' would be, as compared to the economic system we have, which we call 'capitalism'. They go over the history of socialist episodes around the world – Cuba, the Soviet Union, Venezuela, North Korea – and remind us of how disastrous these were, as if this is enough to make us love the present system. But people are not so stupid and ill-informed that they are unaware of these well-known events. Also, they have sufficient confidence in their democratic power to believe they can put 'socialists' in power and stop them going further than some limited basic changes to the present system. For those of us who, like me, think this would be a dangerous risk to take, what we need to do is to fix the capitalist system so socialism seems less attractive to voters. This is an agenda I try to identify in what follows: to explain what has gone wrong and how to fix it.

The last big peacetime crisis of capitalism was created by the Great Depression of the 1930s. The most recent crisis was created by the Great Recession starting in 2008. Now, on top of its aftermath, we have the coronavirus lockdown crisis. After the Great Depression, major changes were made in Western countries' policies, as urged by Keynes. Governments became far more active in fiscal policy in preventing slumps in demand; monetary policy was relegated to a support role, setting interest rates to allow demand to be regulated by fiscal policy. As is now well known, these policies led after World War II to high and persistent inflation, so that today central banks target inflation and fiscal policy is generally held in control to prevent government debt becoming too large.

Today's financial crisis and the Great Recession have in turn forced big changes in Western countries' policies. We have now introduced heavy regulation of bank behaviour, combined with aggressive printing of money at zero or even negative interest rates in the attempt to create renewed growth. Furthermore, these policies have been accompanied by sharp fiscal contraction, with 'austerity' the main fiscal aim of most Western governments. The living standards of Western households have fallen sharply, and it is because of this that there is widespread disappointment with capitalism, fuelling 'populist' revolts such as the election of President Trump and Brexit.

In this chapter, I will look at what caused the Great Recession, how to put a full end to it now, and how to avoid a future one. I will also consider how the despair of ordinary Western households can be alleviated, so persuading them not to back supposedly socialist parties in future elections. I will also consider how governments can respond to the coronavirus crisis.

To anticipate, I will be explaining how it was a failure of monetary policy that caused the Great Recession, and that avoidance of future ones depends on a radical overhaul of monetary policy rules. I will also argue that to put a full end to the Great Recession as it continues to drag on in the form of weak recovery and renewed recession, in spite of continued but ineffectual efforts from monetary policy, we must endorse a self-limiting fiscal expansion, and within it tackle the discontents of average households that now fester, through the reform of government spending and tax policies. Through these measures we will get the capitalist economy of the UK working effectively again and satisfying its critics with this improved performance.

WHAT IS CAPITALISM? WHY IS IT WORTH SAVING?

Capitalism is not best thought of as a 'system', but rather as a set of institutions that allow trial and error by households and firms owned by them in providing supplies to each other. This makes it like an 'algorithm', that is, like a computer programme that endlessly searches across the supply space for the best values. The key institutions contributing to this algorithm are company formation under limited liability, contract law and bankruptcy. These institutions we call the 'market system', in which suppliers are contracted to demanders under legal processes.

Socialism, as is well known, replaces these with central planning/ authority. The problem with this lies in the obvious inability for it to discover the best values the capitalist algorithm discovers. This is because capitalism harnesses the information held by all households and firms in its search processes, while socialism only harnesses the information held by the central planner. It cannot compel households and firms to provide 'full' information because, even if incentives could be created to do so, the central planner defines the needed information but does not have the necessary detailed information to know what the need is. The 'need' is defined by the algorithm in which everyone is involved; without the algorithm, needs are unknown.

Hence, the fundamental issue lies in the information capacity of the two systems, as originally pointed out by Hayek (1944). Even the most benevolent socialist authority, with a hatred of concentration camps and authoritarian methods, will inevitably be frustrated by this information failure.

THE UNNECESSARY FINANCIAL CRISIS

To understand how the financial crisis occurred, we must first consider how monetary policy was conducted until 2008. In the early 1990s, central banks started to embrace inflation targeting, together with associated 'central bank independence' so that supposedly spendthrift governments should not impose inflationary financing on them. These new policies led to a period of low inflation, which in turn we now know from recent research (Le, Meenagh and Minford, 2019) encouraged firms to keep prices and wages stable: price and wage durations lengthened, meaning that output was increasingly dominated by demand shocks because these did not provoke the rise in prices that would have choked off demand and so contained the needed rise in output. This was a 'New Keynesian' world, in the sense that prices and wages did not respond, much as Keynes argued they would not in the modern capitalist world of large companies and powerful unions. As it turned out, the 1990s was an era of moderate demand shocks; also, productivity growth was steadily positive. The era became known as 'the Great Moderation', with low and stable inflation and moderate positive growth. In retrospect, it looks like a time of unusually benign shocks: small demand shocks and positive productivity and other supply shocks.

Here are, according to the Le et al. (2019) estimates, the shares of 'sticky price' sectors (or New Keynesian, NK, weights in labour and goods markets) in the US economy. It can be seen in Figure 5.1 that, by 2007, the shares had reached 90% in response to the Great Moderation, creating maximum vulnerability to the bad demand shock about to be unleashed, due to the huge credit build-up.

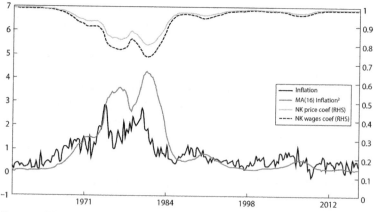

Note: NK = New Keynesian; MA = moving average; RHS = right-hand side.
Source: Le et al. (2019).

Figure 5.1   *Time-varying NK weights (sticky-price shares of goods and labour markets)*

As it proceeded from the 1990s, monetary policy began to encourage strong credit growth, especially in the US. Public policy also entered the mix, with the US government encouraging mortgage loans to poor families, to be underwritten by 'Fannie' and 'Freddie', two public institutions able to buy mortgages. It seemed that with real wages having stagnated, 'getting poor people onto the housing ladder' could be an alternative route for obtaining the 'trickle-down' effect of growth. With low inflation successfully engineered, central banks disregarded the growth in the monetary and credit aggregates that accelerated into the 2000s. As dollars became more plentiful, the People's Bank of China bought them to prevent the yuan appreciating against the dollar; and easy money spread to China through this channel. These developments can be seen in the money growth figures that follow, globally and for the US, China, the eurozone and the UK (Figures 5.2–5.8).

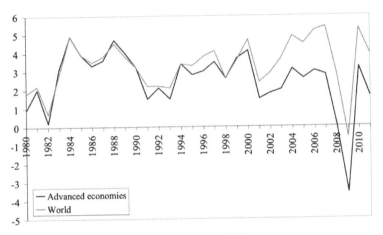

Source: Hodge Bank (2020), *Quarterly Economic Bulletin.*

Figure 5.2   *Real GDP growth (annual percentage change)*

World growth increased, with China reaching 13% at one point; world growth peaked at over 5% and world commodity and oil prices soared as excess capacity was used up. By 2007, these prices had hit high peaks, with oil at $150 a barrel. It was plain that growth must be arrested, if only by lack of resource capacity, even though final prices were slow to generate downstream inflation, with firms still setting long price durations and so reacting slowly to cost increases.

Central banks were finally realizing the threat of rising inflation by 2007 when the mortgage crisis burst, with various banks reporting defaults on their bought-in packages of mortgages. The interbank market

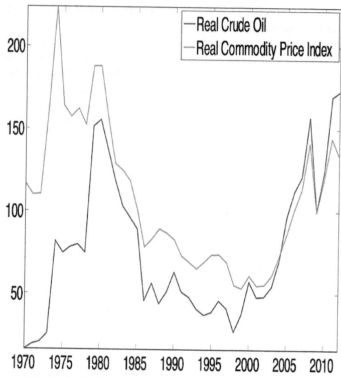

Source: Hodge Bank (2020), *Quarterly Economic Bulletin.*

Figure 5.3   Commodities

seized up, with uncertainty about which banks borrowing in it might be
at risk. Interest rate rises were put on hold and central banks went into
crisis-prevention mode: various banks were rescued by central bank
loans plus concerted takeover by other banks. This early era of bank
bailout created a political backlash, especially among Republicans. It
succeeded in stabilizing bank liquidity so that by the middle of 2008 it
seemed as if a full-scale banking crisis had been averted. Then, out of
the blue, in September 2008, Lehman went bankrupt; shortly afterwards,
AIG, the world's biggest insurance company, went down with it. The
financial crisis had occurred with a vengeance.

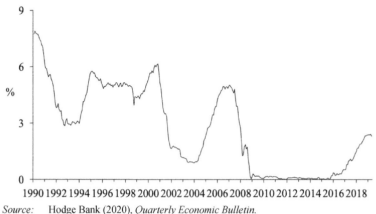

Source: Hodge Bank (2020), *Quarterly Economic Bulletin.*

Figure 5.4   US: Three-month Treasury bill interest rate

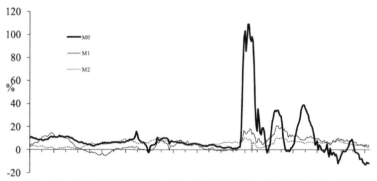

Source: Hodge Bank (2020), *Quarterly Economic Bulletin.*

Figure 5.5   US: Growth in monetary aggregates (year on year)

Could central banks have averted it? The answer is plainly – yes. Lehman could have been saved by a coordinated package of takeovers by other banks (among whom Barclays was keen to buy parts of Lehman) and loans injected by central banks, plus general liquidity provision to the interbank market, where Lehman's problems originated. It seems that central bankers lost their nerve in the face of a political climate increas-

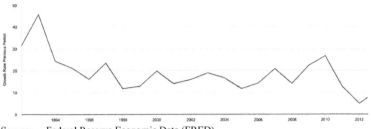

Source: Federal Reserve Economic Data (FRED).

Figure 5.6   Growth of M1 in China

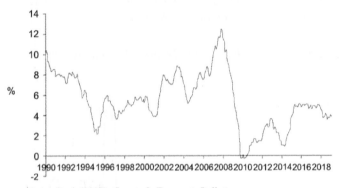

Eurozone M3 Growth

Source: Hodge Bank (2020), *Quarterly Economic Bulletin.*

Figure 5.7   Eurozone M3 growth

ingly hostile to bank bailout, not just in the US but also the UK, where Barclays was expressly forbidden by the UK government from buying Lehman in the talks led by the Fed that attempted to prevent the bankruptcy. Even among central bankers, such as Mervyn King, a school of thought had arisen that banks needed to be taught a lesson, to avoid in future the 'moral hazard' of excessive lending, implicitly supported by the taxpayer. Other banks, whose cooperation was needed in any Lehman package, became increasingly alarmed that if their turn ever came, the central bank willingness to supply money would have run out.

So it was that after long discussions on Sunday, 14 September 2008, Lehman's bankruptcy was finally decided. No action was taken to close

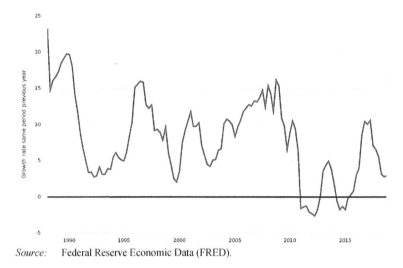

Source: Federal Reserve Economic Data (FRED).

Figure 5.8   M3 for the United Kingdom

markets or provide special assistance. After AIG's bankruptcy, the full savagery of the financial crisis became clear and forced governments to intervene with large taxpayer bailouts, both in the US and the UK. World trade and growth collapsed overnight, as credit lines were extinguished. The Great Recession had begun.

It is plain that central banks could have averted it at two stages. First, monetary policy could have been tightened in the 2000s, so preventing the massive credit boom up to 2007. Second, central banks could have coordinated a rescue of Lehman along earlier lines. However, central bank failure did not stop there. What was needed, given the general banking collapse, was an immediate liquidity injection into the banking system, together with the easing of any restrictions on banks' lending capacity. This could have caused a rapid turnaround from credit blight to credit expansion.

Unfortunately, central banks had taken from this whole episode the moral that banks, not they, had behaved irresponsibly, and that bank regulation should be sharply tightened to prevent future credit expansion to 'risky' clients. The fact that bank clients are in general risky, it being banks' role to extend risky credit, duly escaped central bank thinking under this new view of the need for regulation to 'prevent future crises'.

Plans for this new regulation were drawn up in early 2008 and instead of being put on indefinite hold when the crisis struck in September, they continued to be rolled out and duly prevented the necessary snapback in bank lending.

So, central banks' regulation of banks, rolled out by developed country governments, now became the reason recovery from the crisis was so slow. Of course, for central banks, there was the undoubted consolation that through it all their own bureaucratic role had been massively strengthened, to include bank regulation as well as their continued independent execution of monetary policy.

As part of this enhanced role, central banks developed the new tool of deliberate balance sheet expansion, printing money to acquire large amounts of government debt. This 'quantitative easing' (QE) was an extension of 'open market operations' in debt, but on a greatly expanded scale and in one direction only. The effect of this 'unorthodox' monetary measure has been to raise the prices of certain assets – notably, government bonds and the liabilities of other 'safe' borrowers including large corporations – while failing to stimulate lending to small firms and other risky borrowers. Banks, generally mired in regulative restraints, have expanded credit slowly, and not much to 'risky' clients. Savers have seen their returns on safe assets disappear and this has spurred them to raise the prices of other, near-safe, assets in the hunt for yield. The result has been a corporate environment skewed against risk-taking and new competition: innovation and productivity growth have suffered (Liu, Mian and Sufi, 2019). The Great Distortion began with this new era of zero interest rates, QE and bank regulation.

THE GREAT DISTORTION

We have had the Great Moderation in the 1990s and the Great Recession in the 2010s. This was succeeded at the end of the 2010s by the Great Distortion of financial markets as QE and bank regulation took their toll.

We know that at the macro level of monetary loosening, QE has been effective (e.g., Le et al., 2019), even though interest rates on safe government bonds have been zero, driven down by QE to this zero lower bound set by the zero interest rate on cash. How has QE worked? By driving up the prices of other assets, including long-term bonds demanded by pension funds, equities and corporate bonds of large companies that have low risk. So, for large private sector agents such as these companies it has been cheap to borrow and raise equity. For example, in May 2019, the initial public offering (IPO) of Uber, a company with poor profit prospects and a huge rate of 'cash burn', valued Uber at \$82 billion. Though this has fallen since, it reveals the market's generosity during the zero-bound episode in valuing large corporations. Meanwhile, capital remains expensive for SMEs for whom market risk drives down equity prices, and capital regulation with high SME risk-rating makes banks reluctant to lend.

The effect of all this has been to distort the financial markets in favour of large dominant companies against their smaller competitors. The effect on competition and productivity has been modelled by Liu et al. (2019). Casual observation confirms that large companies now dominate great swathes of industry, and not merely in technology: concentration has never been higher. This can be seen in Figure 5.9 from Liu et al.'s industrial dataset: the relative productivity of the top 5% in the US has soared as long-run interest rates have fallen. This has correlated with a rising profit and share price divergence of the top 5% vs the rest. The regressions of Liu et al. show that the relative share price of the top 5% responds strongly by rising when the interest rate falls, and that this effect strengthens the lower the interest rate starts from. Also, across the Organisation for Economic Co-operation (OECD) countries, productivity growth has slowed sharply, as typified by Figure 5.10 for the US.

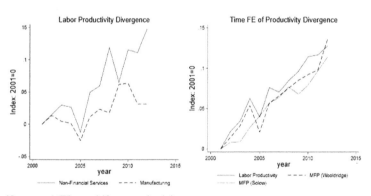

Note: MFP = multifactor productivity.
Source: Liu et al. (2019), Figure A1.

Figure 5.9   *Relative performance of top 5% US firms – widening productivity gap between leaders and followers*

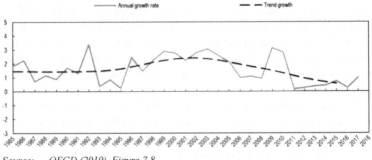

Source: OECD (2019), Figure 7.8.

*Figure 5.10   Labour productivity growth trend, US: total economy,
                 percentage change at annual rate*

THE OVERALL VERDICT ON CENTRAL BANK PERFORMANCE SINCE 2000

In sum, central banks not only caused the Great Recession, first by failing to prevent a credit boom, next by failing to stop the crisis eruption; they also have prevented a rapid recovery from it with their U-turn towards heavy bank regulation. Finally, their 'new monetary tool' of QE has not only been ineffective in stimulating credit/money creation, it has also produced serious market distortion and a productivity slowdown. Central banks have used their new-found independence since the 1990s pretty badly. It is not surprising that their independence is increasingly being questioned after this terrible record of blunders.

The Great Recession has dragged on without being properly ended by sustained growth. Interest rates are still at or close to zero across the Western world – all this before the coronavirus lockdown crisis. The eurozone, having had a bad crisis following on from the US–UK financial crisis, was already close to recession. With central banks having failed to end the Great Recession, what are we to do now, once the virus lockdown is lifted? We go on to discuss this, but first we discuss the impact of the virus crisis.

HOW TO DEAL WITH THE CORONAVIRUS CRISIS: YES, THE GOVERNMENT CAN MANAGE IT EFFECTIVELY

Since the financial crisis aftermath, the world has suddenly been hit by the coronavirus pandemic and the medical need to lock down activity in order to stop its transmission. Since the lockdown necessarily stops economic activity, the question has been how governments can respond via fiscal and monetary policy to palliate the crisis. The challenge has been to preserve people and firms from the income consequences of the lockdown, so that the economy is kept in place and can recover fast when the lockdown is lifted. Plainly, this imposes a large burden on the public finances and the question has been raised as to whether they can in fact afford to do this. In what follows, I will focus on the UK as my main example. But, essentially, the same points apply to any sovereign government, with the potential to issue its own currency.

How Fiscal Policy Copes with Wars and Other Crises – and Now the Coronavirus

To get an understanding of how far the public finances can stretch to cope with national crises, it is helpful to look at UK debt history. Figure 5.11 is from Martin Ellison and Andrew Scott's (2017) article chronicling this. One can see from the upper figure that twice in UK history the market value of debt/GDP has spiked: once in 1830 after the Napoleonic Wars, and once in 1945 after World War II. The first spike was to 200% of GDP, the second to about 150% of GDP. The lower figure is also instructive. It shows the ratio of market/par value of debt. When this is high, interest rates are low, a sign that the government is in a strong position to borrow, probably because the private sector is struggling.

Now look in the lower figure at how the bond market developed as Britain borrowed in the second half of the eighteenth century. The market/par ratio remained at or above unity, as the government built up debt. By the early 1800s, the market/par ratio had fallen sharply. The private economy was resurgent and interest rates rose, devaluing the public debt. One can see a rather similar pattern over World War II debt. As it was accumulated during the war, the market/par ratio remained a bit below unity. By 1950, the ratio had fallen sharply; interest rates had risen as the economy recovered, devaluing the debt.

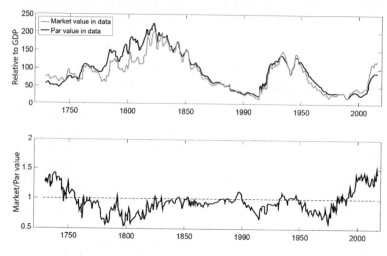

Source: Ellison and Scott (2017), Figure 1.

Figure 5.11   *Market value of debt in UK since 1694; and market/par value*

How were these huge debt ratios paid off? After Napoleon, income tax was introduced. After World War II, inflation devalued debt while taxes were also raised.

Application to the Coronavirus Crisis

Apply this to the coronavirus situation. With lockdown threatening a recession lasting three months or more, the UK government support package has been put at £400 billion as a rough round number, about 20% of GDP. If lockdown goes on for longer, as we must pray it does not, that number will spiral upwards. To understand how high the number could go, we need to do some basic arithmetic on the government accounts. National income or GDP breaks down into tax (40%) and disposable income (60%: roughly 50% accrues to non-taxpayers). Imagine now that GDP falls by 10%. This reduces tax takings by 4% of GDP, and also reduces disposable income. But as disposable income falls, the government pays tax credits (benefits) to the 50% not paying tax: assume their 50% of income falls by 5% of GDP and the tax credit rate is 80% as now promised in the government package. Then government benefits rise by 4% of GDP. The total rise in the fiscal deficit is thus 8% of GDP when GDP falls by 10%. Now consider a lockdown lasting six months: that is, half a year's GDP, a 50% fall on the year 2020 say. The resulting fiscal deficit would then be around 40% of GDP. On top of the UK's existing public debt/GDP ratio of around 80%, this would take the UK ratio to over 100% of GDP, much on a par with the situation post-World War II.

However, the government is greatly assisted by two interlocking factors. Interest rates today are nearly zero, with the yield on ten-year gilts around 0.4%. At the same time, central banks are bound to help out during the crisis by buying gilts and printing money, keeping interest rates at this zero floor. This implies that the government can borrow for next to nothing during the crisis and for very long maturities. But, afterwards, interest rates will rise as the economy recovers, and this rise will lower the repayment burden sharply. To give an arithmetical example, with the UK government's current average debt maturity of 16 years, if the government borrowed £100 billion at today's rates of 0.4% p.a., its market value at post-crisis interest rates of say 5% p.a. would be only £50 billion. This implies that future taxpayers are faced with a much reduced burden of debt to pay off: one can calculate the tax rate needed to pay the debt off as £50 billion times the new interest rate of 5%.

The longer the maturity at which the government borrows, the more favourable this arithmetic, which explains why the UK Debt Management Office has typically favoured long-maturity gilts. Indeed, if it were to reissue all UK debt as indefinitely lasting coupon-paying perpetuities, then £100 billion of that issue would, at a post-crisis interest rate of 5%, fall in value to only £8 billion. If we translate this into the need to pay off 100% debt to GDP contracted by the end of the virus crisis, it turns out the necessary tax rise is just 0.4% of GDP. This could be raised quite easily – just 1.3 pence on the standard rate of income tax.

Another way of explaining this favourable arithmetic is to focus on the interest cost of all this debt after the crisis. The 100% of GDP in debt that would have been raised and rolled over before and during the crisis would have required an interest rate of around 0.4% p.a. So, the interest on it that must be paid by future taxpayers is very low.

Objectively, this is a poor situation, as it is bad for savers and pensioners. But pre-virus policy failed to avoid this, so it is the situation inherited from before the virus struck, about which nothing can be done – savers and pensioners' returns are terrible, whatever is done. The result is that the Treasury can use savers' funds at virtually no cost for this bailout, putting hardly any extra burden on future taxpayers.

It might be asked: should not the Treasury restore the economy to a state where savers get proper returns? In an ideal world, the answer would be yes. But in the world we face, of the ongoing pandemic, the Treasury is unable to do this: returns on all assets have been destroyed by the pandemic, with the economy locked down into severe recession. The process of restoring returns must wait until recovery after the crisis; the policies then should be very different, as we discuss shortly. For now, the Treasury is raising funds from savers who are desperate to lend at virtually any positive interest rate. Its duty is to borrow its needs at the lowest possible cost to the taxpayer. As we have seen, it can do this very cheaply indeed.

One can see from this the powers that governments have as monopoly raisers of taxes and printers of money. During crises when people have nowhere else to put their savings, governments can borrow easily as the only safe deposit show in town, while the taxpayer sits at their back as repayment guarantee. Meanwhile, the central bank can print money, driving down rates of return on all assets, cheapening the cost of public borrowing. What all this implies is that a sovereign government with a reliable taxpaying public is in a powerful position to cope with the financial fall-out from wars and other fiscal crises.

Nevertheless, one must remember that to have a reliable taxpaying public, one must have a functioning economy. That is why the most vital need in this crisis is to find a way to get people back to work, so the economy can revive. In the Appendix to this chapter, written in April 2020, we show in an analysis based on the cross-country data and the robust epidemic descriptive model, the logistic, why lockdown needed to be lifted as soon as possible.

THE FORECAST OUTLOOK AFTER THE CORONAVIRUS CRISIS

Our coronavirus analysis – detailed in the Appendix to this chapter – implies that COVID-19-related deaths will steadily fall away to zero in the UK, in spite of the easing of the lockdown; we see similar developments around the world, summarized in the projection below for a 'global' group of the worst-affected countries (Figure 5.12). This fall-off in deaths will feed into a rise in household confidence about returning to normal behaviour. This underpins our forecasts of a V-shaped recovery, in which a GDP fall in 2020 of about 6.5% is followed by a rise of around 6% in 2021 (Table 5.1). Internationally, we see a similar picture, though with a longer recession in the EU because of its pre-COVID problems. We note that with the COVID crisis itself, what the virus has caused in lockdown the retreat of the virus will reverse.

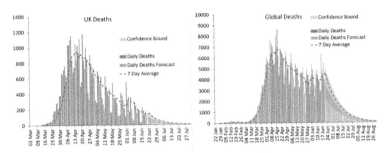

Source: Johns Hopkins University, Coronavirus Resource Center.

Figure 5.12   *UK and global deaths*

Table 5.1   *Forecast of world growth*

Growth of Real Gross Domestic Product (GDP)						
	2017	2018	2019	2020	2021	2022
USA	2.2	2.9	2.3	−6.5	6.0	2.5
UK	1.8	1.4	1.4	−6.4	6.0	2.9
Japan	2.2	0.3	1.0	−6.0	2.3	1.0
Germany	2.5	1.5	0.5	−6.5	5.8	2.0
France	2.4	1.7	1.3	−8.1	2.1	2.0
Italy	1.7	0.8	0.2	−9.9	6.4	1.9

Source: Hodge Bank (2020), *Quarterly Economic Bulletin.*

Policy must also look to the future, and any possible entirely new wave of infection from a mutated virus. We can predict how the virus's behaviour will evolve towards that of a normal flu. Future waves should have a lower Infection Fatality Rate, IFR or death rate per infected person, the more deadly strains having partly died out with their hosts. This suggests that we can use our estimated model for future waves, but updated for a much lower death rate, like that of a normal flu at around 0.1%, an eighth of what the UK has experienced in the current wave.

HOW TO HANDLE FISCAL AND MONETARY POLICY AFTER THE CRISIS

Now turn to the moment the economy is released from the virus lockdown and starts to recover. Some commentators, such as Anatole Kaletsky (https://citywire.co.uk/funds-insider/news/anatole-kaletsky-we -need-a-massive-helicopter-drop-of-qe-to-save-the-british-economy/ a1335693), have argued for continued monetary and fiscal stimulus, to push the economy all the faster to normal. They have suggested that this would run no risks with inflation. However, this is bad advice. It is true that inflation has been quiescent for a decade while there have been substantial fiscal deficits in spite of austerity programmes and money has been printed on a massive scale by central banks through their QE programmes. Essentially, highly expansionary monetary policy has failed to prevent a world of moderate deflation. Yet, it was a series of mistakes made by central banks that led to this outcome, as set out above. First, they fed a credit boom in the 2000s, then as bank balance sheets weakened with rising non-performing loans, they allowed Lehman to go bankrupt, precipitating the banking crisis. After the huge consequential bailouts, when bank credit needed to expand rapidly to create recovery, central banks brought in draconian new rules for banks that stopped them lending. Their ensuing QE programme duly failed to trigger the upsurge in bank credit and broad money that was intended. Instead, it drove interest rates down to zero and drove up other asset prices. In the aftermath of the coronavirus crisis, it is vital these mistakes are not repeated.

Coming out of the crisis, the government will hold large chunks of private equity. And banks will hold large portfolios of credit in private firms that have survived the crisis. In practice, the draconian regulations restraining bank credit creation will have been lifted. To prevent a huge surge in money and credit growth, the government must sell off its private equity stakes and central banks must sell off their massive holdings of government bonds to contract the money supply. This is necessary to prevent a serious inflation from taking hold.

It is easy to be complacent about the inflationary effects of large-scale money printing. The Weimar Republic, faced with a weak economy, low tax revenues and French demands for reparations, printed money to fill their fiscal gap. Because there are lags before the resulting expansion of credit and broad money affects demand and confidence in money, the Weimar government was initially happy with the results of this policy. But it was soon fuelling the most terrible hyperinflation, which ruined the economy.

With the government still running fiscal deficits until the economy recovers, there will continue to be substantial fiscal stimulus. With demand surging relative to a supply still getting going, prices will rise. Provided money is kept under control, interest rates will rise as well, and we will gradually return to a normal monetary environment, with interest rates around 5% and inflation controlled at around 2–3%, in line with the targets that central banks are committed to.

The final question to be answered is: how should fiscal policy progress after the crisis? Some illustrative figures can help us with our thinking. Plainly, the UK government will emerge with a large debt/GDP ratio after the crisis package has been rolled out. Suppose it costs £500 billion, on top of existing debt of around 80% of GDP (now around £2000 billion), which we can assume is being refinanced at current low interest rates as far as possible, and also at the longest possible maturities. That would together imply a total debt of £2100 billion at par, having been issued by the end of 2020, some 100% of GDP. Let us assume as above that by 2022 interest rates have risen to about 5%, with gradually tightening monetary conditions. This would imply that at market value, debt would only be 8% of GDP. What we are seeing here is that debt interest being so low on the debt that was issued, its being discounted at interest rates some ten times higher than at issue, its market value is greatly reduced. These figures reveal that 'fiscal re-entry' is reasonably manageable after the crisis.

If we consider the steady state spend and tax situation post-crisis, it looks like this:

- ongoing public spending: 40% of GDP;
- ongoing debt interest: 0.4% of GDP (on the par debt issue of 100% of GDP, issued at an interest rate of 0.4%);
- ongoing required tax revenue: 40.4% of GDP;
- fiscal adjustment required via higher taxes to raise current tax/GDP ratio from around 40% to 40.4%.

These figures for the UK can be paralleled in other developed countries, all of which have the sovereign power to borrow and print money. This is true even in the EU where only the European Central Bank (ECB) can print money; sovereign governments have the power to borrow but the ECB has shown itself very willing to buy the resulting government bonds by printing money, creating a broadly similar situation to that in the US or the UK.

So, what we have seen here is that the fiscal inheritance from the coronavirus lockdown crisis is entirely manageable with quite small tax rises, simply because borrowing will take place at nugatory interest rates. No doubt there will be those that urge austerity to bring down high par debt/GDP ratios. But, as we have explained, these are no guide to the necessary fiscal adjustment. The market value of debt to GDP will be very much lower, reflecting the way that very low interest payment streams will be discounted at the newly normal interest rates. In the next section we go on to explain how this can be brought about once the virus lockdown is over.

HOW TO DIG THE WORLD ECONOMY, ONCE OUT OF VIRUS LOCKDOWN, OUT OF THE GREAT RECESSION CREATED BY CENTRAL BANK MISTAKES

The state of the world economy, regardless of the virus lockdown, can only be described as weak and lacking in confidence, with low productivity growth. Interest rates on safe assets like government bonds range from zero on short-dated paper to a maximum of around 2% on very long-term bonds, but close to zero on most Western countries' long-term bonds, with the US at around 2% as the only exception. In Japan and the eurozone, all rates are close to zero, while rates paid to banks on their central bank balances are actually negative. On risky assets, rates are generally positive, reflecting the risk premium; however, as noted above, large corporations enjoying dominant market positions are able to access capital at close to zero cost, which is heavily distorting market competition. As for governments, they can raise capital at negative real interest rates, implying that they are being paid to borrow; they can even print money to finance themselves at negative real interest rates. These facts signal that desperate times are with us. Monetary policy is a busted flush, with its latest tool, QE, actually damaging the situation. Can nothing be done?

The clue to what can be done is to be found in the statement just above: that people will pay governments to borrow and spend. This mirrors the desperate plight of the private sector, unwilling to borrow enough at such low interest rates that the economy would surge and raise the rate of return to normal.

Because of the bailouts of banks and related financial costs, Western governments have historically high debt/GDP ratios. Yet, because of QE, as much as a third of this debt is actually simply money – the debts have been bought by central banks in return for printed money. In normal times we would worry that all this printed money would cause inflation; and we would be urging the central banks to sell their bonds and retrieve the money. Yet, plainly, we are not in normal times. It is as if people were going around too emaciated to eat large stores of accumulated food that in normal times we would worry might cause obesity. The economy is too emaciated to use the huge supplies of money that have been printed.

Abnormal times require abnormal solutions. Fortunately, all Western countries have governments that can borrow, spend and cut taxes. As we have seen, they can do this at negative cost in debt interest; this means that future taxpayers will gain from the negative real interest cost on the debt, effectively only paying back less than the real value of the debt. From society's viewpoint, provided the government can get a social return on its spending or its tax cuts that is positive, then this borrowing pays. Future taxpayers will have more income with which to pay off less than 100% of the debt. This means that there is no argument to be had with future taxpayers. Meanwhile, current taxpayers will plainly be delighted if the government would take this action, bringing immediate direct benefits, but more importantly restoring the economy to functionality and confidence.

For those who feel concerned about adding to public debt ratios for fears of insolvency, this arithmetic provides consolation. The truth is that if such fiscal policies work and push up interest rates once more to the normal real interest rates of the past, then any current rise in debt ratios will actually be reversed. Here is a simple arithmetical example of what can happen – repeated from our analysis above of the coronavirus deficits. Suppose a country starts off with a debt ratio of 100%, of which say a third is very long-term debt, say perpetuities, with long-term interest rates at 1% p.a. Now assume it spends 10% of GDP borrowing on more very long-term bonds to spend and cut taxes, and that this in time drives interest rates up to 3%. Its new stock of long-term bonds will go up at first to 43% of GDP. But once interest rates rise to 3%, its value will fall by a third to 14% of GDP; this is because it is now being discounted by a rate three times higher than the current 1% (the value of a perpetuity is the coupon paid each year divided by the rate of interest). It therefore strongly pays governments with long-term debts to get long-term interest rates back up to normal, in the interests of solvency alone.

This example also shows that fiscal expansionism in these troubled times will bring its own termination and so can be thought of as self-limiting. Once interest rates get back up to normal, the normal solvency calculus will apply. New borrowing will once again be expensive in real terms; and potential movements in interest rates downwards will threaten yet higher future debt values and should induce the usual caution over fiscal deficits.

It is important to realize that the case I am making here for fiscal expansion is strictly exceptional, to be ended once normality returns. It echoes Hayek's response to Keynes's work, *The General Theory of Employment, Interest and Money* (1936); Hayek agreed that, in the very special circumstances of a stubborn depression, fiscal stimulus could be justified, but he said there was not a 'general' case for fiscal 'activism', which Keynes was arguing for, on the grounds that the unaided economy might repeatedly fall into this state (Caldwell, 1998). The same is true here. Usually, the economy works well without fiscal intervention. Any needs for stabilization can be supplied by monetary policy. What has happened, however, is that monetary policy has laid waste the economy's usual robustness by dreadful mistakes, leaving only fiscal policy as the tool for the restoration of its robustness that we desperately need.

I leave on one side here the details of what spending, what tax cuts and how great in total borrowing should be in the rest of the world. I would simply commend President Trump's tax cuts and urge Congress to agree with Trump a large infrastructure programme. In the eurozone, I would urge a general liberalization of fiscal policy, backed up by an ECB pledge to buy the bonds of any government facing market pushback; in particular, I would urge the German government to abandon its doctrinal opposition to fiscal deficits, at least until the Great Recession is over.

For the UK, Brexit is an excuse for a radical new direction in policy, to be backed up by fiscal liberalism. In a later chapter we will go on to discuss some detailed projections for the UK. What is clear is that capitalist governments have here a good opportunity to demonstrate their power to enhance living standards by well-targeted spending and tax cuts that raise spending power and strengthen corporate competitiveness.

Assuming we have revived the world economy with a large dose of fiscal expansion and got world interest rates back up to a normal 5% or so, we can go on to implement the post-Brexit policies needed in coming decades. We now turn to these issues of Brexit, beginning with trade and regulative issues where our departure from the EU creates the most immediate opportunities for policy change. Furthermore, with interest rates back up to a normal range, well away from the zero lower bound, we can review the way monetary policy is conducted, to make sure we have no repeat of the financial crisis and the zero bound. That is a topic we will explore in some detail in Chapter 6.

APPENDIX: MODELLING AND FORECASTING CORONAVIRUS BEHAVIOUR (CO-AUTHORED WITH DAVID MEENAGH)

When expert epidemiologists disagree so much about the progress of the coronavirus, why should mere economists suggest a new way to forecast the virus's progress? Two reasons. The first is that economists are familiar with the way the whole family of 'epidemic' processes will show up in the data, so that it is likely that progress can be directly estimated; this is the 'logistic' S-shaped descriptive model we will set out shortly. The second is that the economic damage of the main medical intervention so far, lockdown, is so massive that this debate just cannot be left to the disputes of medical experts – it is far from just a medical matter. Likely virus progress must be reliably juxtaposed against likely economic cost, to get the resulting policy judgement right. In this Appendix, we explain how we have modelled the progress of the virus and concluded that lockdown should really have been replaced with social guidance as adopted in Sweden.

We begin by applying the logistic function, which is how epidemic behaviour plays out in the data of infections, to the data for deaths from COVID-19, for the UK and Sweden, which we chose because it followed different policies, especially on lockdown. We have then set out a causal model of the COVID virus behaviour based on evolutionary biology and the optimizing reactions of households. We have estimated and tested this by indirect inference, matching its simulated logistic behaviour to that found in the data. Using these model estimates, our policy finding is that the general public health policies pursued in Sweden were more effective than their UK equivalent in their effects on the death rate from infections, while the UK lockdown was no more effective than Swedish advisory policies in reducing the virus's spread, but the cost in loss of GDP was much lower in Sweden.

1   **Describing the data – the logistic curve**

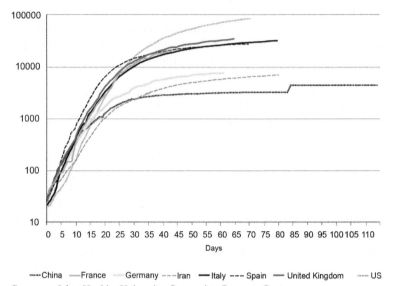

-----China ——France ----Germany ---Iran ——Italy --- Spain —— United Kingdom -----US

Source: Johns Hopkins University, Coronavirus Resource Center.

Figure A5.1   Confirmed deaths by day since total passed 20

The progress of coronavirus infections – the deaths they cause – shown
in Figure A5.1 – plotted on a log (i.e., proportional) scale – reveal
a common and coherent pattern, which comes from an underlying
'logistic stock-flow' model of the virus; such a model is widely used to
project how innovations spread through a population – whether it is new
ideas, new technologies, or, as here, infections. Imagine that you have
a population free of the virus, ranged from those with easy infectability
at the one end to some at the other with great immunity. Enter the virus,
with a mechanism of transmission from person to person via coughing,
touching and so on. In the initial slow stage, the virus will take time to
infect a substantial group. In the second rapid stage, there will be a high
speed of infection as the susceptible will quickly catch it and pass it on
to other susceptible people of whom many are available. At this point the
virus's reproductive rate (R0) will be high, with each infection leading
to several others in a short time. The progress will look 'exponential'

(an exponential curve grows without limit), but it is not, because there is a further stage.

As the stock of infected people accumulates, the virus needs to spread to people with greater natural immunity. The rate of infection (the flow of new infections) and that R0 rate will slow. As the stock of infected people reaches the last tranche of people with the highest immunity, the rate will gradually fall to a stop. In the end, the whole infectable population will have the virus or have had it.

These three stages – initial infection, rapid spread through widely available cases, and finally slowing in the face of saturation – must occur regardless of the epidemiological details. These details show up in the estimated parameters of the describing logistic curve, which therefore is a representation in the data for all epidemics and similar population-penetrating processes, whatever their causal details. The logistic parameters are: the maximum penetration, the rate of infection and the point of inflection where saturation starts to set in. The problem for epidemiological models is that so little is known about this virus. But with the logistic curve we can observe for many countries what these estimated parameters, which reflect this unknown virus's character, are. From this diverse experience we can estimate the likely progression here in the UK, and also the effects of lockdown, the policy now being fiercely debated. Batista (2020) and Golinski and Spencer (2020) have estimated logistic models for various countries.

We fitted a logistic curve to UK and other country reported cases and deaths from COVID-19 from 31 January 2020 to 14 April 2020 (Table A5.1). The logistic function is of the form:

$$f(x, a, b, c) = \frac{c}{1 + e^{-(x-b)/a}}$$

where x is time, and the three parameters are:
a, the infection speed;
b, the day when the maximum number of new infections occurred;
c, the total number of recorded infected people at the end of the infection.

But we can do more by building the structural (i.e., causal) model of virus behaviour that underlies this logistic 'reduced form'. This structural model, if empirically reliable, can give us an understanding of how policy interventions affect the virus's progress. However, we need a means to

Table A5.1 Logistic curve estimation (standard errors in parentheses)

	a	b	c	Population	Deaths/ Population (%)
UK	4.43	36	15 694	66 460 340	0.0236
	(0.08)	(0.20)	(303)		
China (Hubei)	6.70	26	3 165	59 020 000	0.0054
	(0.10)	(0.12)	(0.9)		
US	4.49	0.41	34 345	326 687 500	0.0105
	(0.06)	(0.17)	(572)		
Italy	6.26	38	21 982	60 421 760	0.0364
	(0.12)	(0.20)	(245)		
Spain	4.86	30	18 843	46 796 540	0.0403
	(0.12)	(0.19)	(246)		
France	4.51	52	18 336	66 977 110	0.0274
	(0.08)	(0.16)	(248)		
Germany	4.42	29	3 859	82 905 780	0.0047
	(0.11)	(0.23)	(77)		
Iran	7.52	39	4 986	81 800 270	0.0061
	(0.22)	(0.39)	(94)		

Note: Data up to 14 April 2020 – later series than used above for UK. Logistic curve estimation (standard errors in parentheses).
Source: Author calculations. Population data from World Bank (2018 figures).

establish the model's empirical reliability. For this we use the method of indirect inference where we check the model's capacity to generate the resulting logistic behaviour we observe in the data. This fairly unfamiliar method gives us substantial power to discriminate against inaccurate or mis-specified models. Hence, our account of the virus's logistic progress is not intended to replace the careful modelling of the detailed causal processes driving the virus epidemic; rather, it is intended to describe the data behaviour of the virus's progress. A structural model of the virus's behaviour, which we develop below, can guide us on the effects of policy interventions such as lockdowns. Medical interventions, such as drugs and vaccines, require medical research, which is being energetically pursued by clinical companies in search of a vaccine and effective drug treatments. But, so far, none have been found or used except experimentally. Apart from financing and encouraging this pursuit, governments have intervened in two main ways: first, by attempted denial of entry of the virus into uninfected populations through testing, tracing and quarantining; and second, by lockdown of infected populations. The first has been used by Singapore and South Korea rather effectively. Other countries tried it for a time, the UK among them, but ineffectively, with general popular interaction releasing the virus into general circulation in spite of their efforts. The second intervention of lockdown then has had a plainly visible impact – namely, in slowing the early rate of infection and delaying the point of inflection in time. Against this background, structural model estimates can give us practical guidance on what will happen from what has happened so far. This guidance can help to assess orders of magnitude for future cases and deaths, which is important when one major clinical group, at Imperial College London, have predicted that deaths would have reached half a million had lockdown not occurred and will reach nearly 50 000 even with the lockdown in place since late March.

2   The Rationale of a Causal Model

We now develop a structural model of the coronavirus's behaviour. Our intention is to test and estimate this model by indirect inference, in which we compare the model's simulated behaviour with actual data behaviour and evaluate the match statistically. We will fit it to data for the UK and Sweden, with the aim of identifying differential policy effects between the two countries, both in terms of lockdown and general public health protection; in both, policies differed starkly enough for us to identify the effects with moderate precision. In future work, these methods could be extended to other countries to evaluate the effects of the wide variety of policies they all followed.

In our structural model we treat the coronavirus as having an optimized strategy for infecting a population it has been donated by chance to infect. We can think of this optimization as having been crafted by natural selection over a long period of evolution; in other words, today's virus has evolved to survive because its strategy has been optimized for survival. These ideas belong partly to evolutionary biology (Nesse et al., 2010) and partly to recent dynamic stochastic general equilibrium (DSGE) modelling in macroeconomics (Le et al., 2011) where agents are treated as if they are optimizing strategic decision-makers; here the virus is treated as an optimizing agent whose strategy has been selected by mutation and evolution. We think of the virus as having mutated by natural selection over previous episodes of contact with populations. However, we are currently modelling a particular episode's population that constitutes a new environment, with differences from the previous ones. We divide this environment into elements the virus cannot control but must simply react to, due to the 'surprises' in the current population: these include the death rate, which will reflect the particular make-up of the population (e.g., more or fewer old and unhealthy people), and detailed shocks introduced, for example, by other diseases present and policies adopted by governments. The virus adopts reactions to these elements that reflect behaviour that has proved optimal for evolution to maximize surviving viruses: this maximand is its 'utility'. Furthermore, following the suggestion of Cochrane (2020), we will include people in the model who also act strategically to avoid the costs the virus generates.

We must first go through the biology of susceptibility, infection and recovery, which is used in SIR models (Atkeson, 2020) usually with fixed parameters that define a mechanical progress of the virus. 'S' are those people susceptible to being infected. If infected, they become 'I' people. Having been infected, they then after some time either die or develop powerful enough antibodies to kill the virus; or finally they may recover without killing the virus, so that the virus continues in them in a co-existing state, and they remain susceptible to further infection; those who die or recover and kill the virus are denoted 'R' (recovered) people.

Hence, the virus's utility rises with the expected number infected who have not either died or killed off the virus in recovery. These represent all living clusters of the virus, so we assume it is aiming for as many living virus clusters as possible at any future point of time. As it is infinitely lived, with time preference and risk aversion, it gives value to all these future clusters, discounted by its time preference and in logs, reflecting its risk aversion (diminishing marginal utility of its 'consumption'). It plans on an infinite life, surviving to infect a future population that may be donated to it. We assume there is some cost of the speed of infection; we think of this as due to increasing infection 'effort', which in turn represents the rising risk of policy resistance by the population the faster the infection rate – for example, the faster development of vaccine or drugs that will kill the virus. The biology of the actual infection speed implies that the higher the infected proportion of the population, the slower it is, and we add the effects of social reaction and policy intervention, such as shifts in lockdowns. These effects and the existing rate of infection increase the cost to the virus of achieving infection.

The usual epidemiological model treats infection rates as exogenous to the virus. It then introduces population characteristics and calculates the interaction of the infection rates with these characteristics in an essentially mechanical way (Atkeson, 2020, surveys these SIR group models). In these models, the key parameter is the rate at which the infected I group who have not recovered or died (the R group) pass the virus on to the uninfected susceptible group, S; this parameter can be directly controlled by lockdown and other measures controlling people's interactions. However, this is to treat the virus as unresponsive to circumstances, which would plainly endanger its survival chances. The optimizing framework we use here assumes the virus responds in the best way for its ultimate success in surviving. Beenstock and Dai (2020) point out there are large variations in contagion rates across countries and over time.

It may seem puzzling that a virus, lacking consciousness, can 'respond'. However, this 'response' is simply the result of evolution in the behaviour of surviving mutations. Any given virus at one time will consist of many surviving strains, each infecting in a different way. For example, we know that a rather weak strain, producing weak symptoms, spreads quickly via 'superspreaders'. On the other hand, the highly virulent strain that hospitalizes people tends to die out, as people either recover with strong antibodies or die. When people self-isolate, the virus stops spreading in the blocked channels but continues to spread via channels still open, such as superspreader chains. This is pre-programmed reactivity from the virus, picked up in our model as optimizing behaviour. As we will see, in our model here, the contagion rate is affected by both known and unknown factors, responding to these as stochastic elements. Our approach allows us to estimate a complete structural model of virus behaviour and test it powerfully (see Monte Carlo experiment below) against a reduced form of the data behaviour that we know to be a logistic curve process. By estimating model parameters and the exogenous shocks, we can identify, from different countries' estimated behaviour, policy effects on death rates and on the parameters of the virus's response to the environment. This allows us to estimate the effects of a range of policy interventions – such as the huge variety adopted across many different countries – rather than simply those directly controlling people's interactive behaviour. The model tells us that the daily infection rate responds inversely to the current self-isolation efforts of the population, and the existing (lagged) share of infected population, offsetting these in order to keep the costs of infection smooth over time, while still ensuring that the population gets steadily infected, ensuring new infections indefinitely.

We now insert household behaviour into the model. We will assume that household utility is reduced by infection but also by the personal inconvenience of avoiding infection by self-isolation. This rises directly with the extent of it, and rises indirectly the more uninfected people there are, as this lowers the personal risk of infection from participating, which raises the net costs of self-isolating (the economic costs net of the gain in lower infection risk). There is also a preference error. Households determine a social reaction strategy, including social distancing, self-isolation and hygiene in response to the infection rate.

The model is fitted to deaths. Unfortunately, we do not have data on the actual infections, because tests have not been good enough to estimate these reliably. However, the model gives us estimates of total infection rates, the death rate, infection growth rates and the reporting ratio that are consistent with the actual data. We report these below.

This structural model of the virus's progress is thus derived from the virus's own programming by its evolved biology, by government policies such as lockdown and by households' social actions to contain the disease. The intuition is that as the infected population share gets higher, infection becomes harder and the infection rate drops.

3   Basic Calibration to Available Data from Surveys

In recent weeks, survey data has become available on the numbers in total infected by the virus in the UK and Sweden according to antibody tests that check whether people were infected two to three weeks before, this being the period of antibody production. This data combined with data on deaths gives us a strong estimate of the death rate per infection, the infection fatality rate (IFR), a key parameter of the model.

One widely held hope among virologists opposed to lockdown, such as Professor Carl Heneghan at Oxford and Anders Tegnell, the state epidemiologist in Sweden, was that a majority of the population had contracted the virus without getting more than weak symptoms. This would imply that there was close to herd immunity. This hope has been dashed by available surveys of specific COVID-19 antibody prevalence in several countries, which turns out to be low, in the range of 5–7% here, in Sweden and in Spain, with big cities like London, Stockholm and Madrid reaching 20% or less. Outside big cities large numbers of small areas have had prevalence close to zero. The latest medical research finds that only seriously infected people develop antibodies (Cervia et al., 2020) and that another 40–60% of the population already have general immunity to coronaviruses (Grifoni et al., 2020) and so may have repelled weak infections. So, our models are effectively analysing what causes serious COVID-19 infection in a population without specific defence against it.

If we take a figure of 7% for end-May in both the UK and Sweden, this would imply an IFR of 0.0054 in Sweden, and one of 0.0083 for the UK. We calibrate our models with these two rates, and search for estimates in the region of these.

4   Results of Testing the Model on Data for the UK and Sweden

To understand how the model works, consider the hurdles faced by the virus, all of which are reflected in its utility function. First, there is the death rate, inherited from its evolution through whatever species it has inhabited. Second, there is the measure of how far speed of infection provokes increasing resistance from people with increasing immunity. This parameter is largely set by the population structure – the proportions of types, such as by age, fitness and existing health – since the faster the infection rate, the higher the proportion of people with immunity that the virus will be attempting to infect. Third, there is the measure of how far the proportion of uninfected people in the population stimulates the rate of spread. This is policy related, in that targeting or lockdown arrests the spread to the uninfected. Fourth, there is the household parameter, measuring how households react to the risk of getting the virus by self-isolating, social distancing, hygiene and so on. Finally, there is the constant, which measures the population proportion that will eventually be infected. This is partly related to population structure, partly to government policy and household reactions in stopping the spread via lockdown, track/trace/isolate, and self-isolation. These factors determine the speed with which the virus spreads and also the extent to which it will spread in the end. The model is matched to the logistic data behaviour of deaths.

The viral rate of spread depends directly on how many are uninfected and a joint ratio of the parameters measuring the stimulus of the unin-fected population share (reducing lockdown and reactivity) relative to the resistance from population immunity and reactivity as infection increases. The higher this ratio, then when many in the population are uninfected, the spread is faster. The measure is similar in both countries. Hence, in both, the virus spread fast and has by now infected about 7% of the population according to the model. Effectively, lockdown and social resistance are close substitutes in their effect on virus prevalence.

Table A5.2   *Structural model parameter estimates*

	UK	Sweden	Global
Death rate per infection	0.0084	0.0052	0.0015
Lockdown parameter	4.11	0.151	2.55
Resistance	59.53	40.59	79.02
Social reaction	0.17	2.95	0.62
Spread speed	0.07	0.07	0.04
% population infected to date	7	7	7
% population infected long term	7	7	7
Reported/actual infections (inverse)	0.0499	0.0442	0.0337
	(20)	(23)	(30)
P-value	0.93	0.82	0.70

Source: Author calculations.

As can be seen from Table A5.2, the death rate is lower in Sweden, at 0.0052 vs 0.0084 in the UK. This lower death rate is presumably associated with general public health policies that were more effective in protecting vulnerable groups with the high death rates; the UK's problems with personal protective equipment supplies in hospitals and with care home conditions have been well publicized.

Both the predictions of the number of infections are around 7% of the population long term – low prevalence in line with the latest surveys of antibody presence. The models both imply that actual infections are a large multiple of reported ones: about 20 times here and 23 times in Sweden. This is lower than the results from SIR estimates fitted to data on tests by Dimdore-Miles and Miles (2020), who find that totals including asymptomatic cases relative to tested/reported cases are likely to be considerably higher, with a ratio in the UK of 250. Their results are also consistent with recent estimates from the University of Manchester (2020) based on local authority data that 'over 25%' will have been infected across the UK, taking account of unreported cases. Rather similar findings – of high UK prevalence by end-March – are made in a recent SIR model study of Italian and UK data by the Oxford group led by Professor Sunetra Gupta (Lourenço et al., 2020). However, as we have seen, these predictions are out of line with the latest survey evidence on prevalence.

Our results on the infection rate are reasonably in line with the latest Office for National Statistics (ONS) pilot survey of currently newly infected people, testing positive on a swab test, which it estimates at 0.17–0.4% of the population (ONS, 2020). The model currently predicts about 2400 daily reported cases, which lasting for a total period of 21 days would imply about 51 000 existing known cases in the population, just under 0.1% of the population.

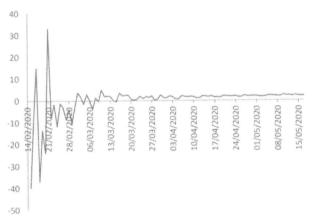

Source: Author calculations.

Figure A5.2   Innovations for the εt process

Our results fit well statistically, as can be seen in Table A5.2. The match of the model to the logistic estimates is good with p-values (the probability that the data does not reject the model); 0.82 for Sweden and 0.93 for the UK. Nevertheless, there is randomness and uncertainty at work. The error term (Figure A5.2) measures the variability in the model's behaviour, which comes from biological and other (mostly policy) shocks to the rate of infection. The consequence of these shocks for the behaviour of deaths is that the simulated histories (Figure A5.3) for the UK vary substantially and are far from the smooth progressions imputed by the logistic curve.

Shown below are the simulated 2.5% probability bounds on the logistic parameters for the UK, which arise from this variability. Faced with spikes like these, it is not surprising that governments were driven to use drastic lockdowns to make sure of suppression. Fitting a logistic function to the deaths data results in the parameters shown in Table A5.3. The bounds shown come from the simulated variation from the structural model – not from the logistic estimates on the data, which are rather tightly estimated, as listed above. They are indicating that a wide variety of logistic models could emerge from the structural model with some probability. The logistic model estimated on the UK deaths data is highly probable with a p-value of 0.93, as we have seen.

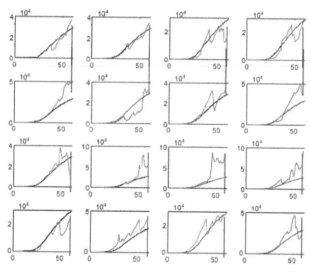

Source: Author calculations.

Figure A5.3   Illustrative simulations of deaths

We also fitted the model to data for a 'global' average of all countries that had deaths of more than 1500 – 25 in all. Our main policy focus is on Sweden and the UK because they provide us with a benchmarking ability. The global model estimates are of interest as an additional test of the model's plausibility. The countries included spanned a huge variety of government policies, but according to the model this should not make much difference to outcomes since social reaction substitutes closely for government policy, effectively offsetting it in the resulting equilibrium. This is what we find. The parameter measuring government reaction lies above Sweden and below the UK; the parameter of social reaction mirrors this, lying below Sweden and above the UK. According to the model, there is more natural resistance in these countries than in either the UK or Sweden, with a high parameter. The rate of spread is correspondingly slower. The global model is calibrated so that a similar long-term proportion of people should be infected globally as in the UK and Sweden.

Table A5.3   *The auxiliary model estimates and bounds are for the logistic curve, as fitted for UK data*

	Actual	Lower 2.5%	Upper 2.5%	Mean
a	10.2775	2.2953	20.8867	8.3010
b	47.4228	30.8611	77.5785	46.2417
c	3 838.1847	18 601.3551	89 002.1526	40 782.6827

Source: Author calculations.

The herd immunity puzzle
The progress of the virus should stop naturally at the point of herd immunity. It has generally been thought that this point is reached when about 60% of the population has been infected. However, what our model estimates are indicating is that this point is being reached at much lower infection rates, more like 7%. How could this be the case? A key parameter is the reaction of people to the infection as it grows. This parameter triggers social distancing when the virus strikes a community, much as a herd of antelope reacts by running as a group when a predatory lion pack is spotted. If this parameter is put at zero, the herd immunity estimate is close to the usual 60%. But, as suggested by Cochrane (2020), social responses bring it right down. The population is responding to information rationally as it arrives, in a rational expectations equilibrium.

We now go on to consider the implications for policy of the model estimates.

5   Policy Implications of the Model Estimates

We can now discuss the experience of the two countries and the different estimates we get from them for these factors. From this we can learn a fair amount about the effectiveness and costs of different government policies. Our main focus in the policy discussion that follows is on the UK, using Sweden as the main identifying benchmark, for outcomes of alternative policies, of no lockdown but instead information and advice on social distancing, together with other general public health policies.

Comparing the UK and Sweden we find that the parameter of natural resistance to the virus's rate of progression is much the same, but the Swedish IFR is substantially lower. This will be related to the effectiveness of controlling the access of the disease to vulnerable groups, like the ill and elderly; the better the protection against infection within hospitals and care homes, the less this access. In the UK, problems with PPE in the NHS and care homes have, as noted earlier, been well publicized.

Also, the Swedish estimate, reflecting social reaction, is much higher than in the UK, where it is close to zero, while the parameter reflecting government-imposed policies like lockdown is around zero in Sweden, much lower than in the UK. These two parameters are, of course, close substitutes, since the social reaction compensates for lack of policy reaction.

Our interest in policy lies particularly in the effect of the UK lockdown. According to our model, this is found in the policy-reaction parameter. However, as we have seen, the higher this parameter, the lower the social reaction parameter; there is strong substitution. It is the two together that determine the equilibrium progress of the virus, both its end infected share of the population and its rate of spread. The model suggests that there is no difference in the behaviour of the virus between the two economies. We can illustrate this clearly from the data for both in Figure A5.4.

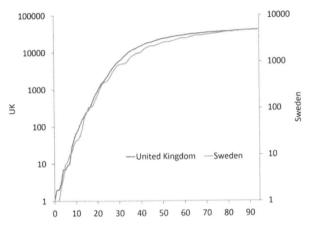

Figure A5.4   Cumulative confirmed deaths (log scale)

The implication is that lockdown achieved nothing extra compared with what a decentralized social reaction strategy, as pursued in Sweden, would have achieved. We could assume that the Swedish and UK relative policy costs are reflected in the relative consensus forecasts made in September 2020 for their 2020 GDP fall: for Sweden this is 4.3%, but for the UK it is 10.1%, 5.8% more. According to the model, lockdown saved no deaths but...a GDP loss of more than £100 billion. Plainly, relying on social responses as in Sweden would have been far more cost-effective than lockdown, for much the same outcome in deaths. We do not need to appeal to any cost per life saved as in transport policy where typically £11 million per life saved is used as a benchmark;[1] the point is that lockdown has cost a lot for no lives saved.

However, the Swedish experience suggests that other policies, of a general public health nature, succeeded in reducing deaths by lowering the death rate. Had Swedish health policies been applied in the UK, the population infected would have been the same but the death rate 0.003% lower at 0.056%. UK deaths would have been about 26 000, some 14 000 less than the current total.

Current UK policy aims to lift the lockdown but introduce stringent test/trace/isolate policies of localized lockdown – 'whack-a-mole' – stopping localized outbreaks fast. However, the Swedish experience suggests that decentralized social reaction will do the same job without this heavy-handed government action. All that the government needs to contribute is any information it can provide, such as from surveys and local hospital reports: the people will do the rest. Given that there are random shocks to the model, we can think of these as random starts of mini-waves; however, they provoke social reactions that bring the case and deaths outcomes back to the equilibrium path.

Conclusion

In this Appendix we have fitted the logistic function, the reduced form of epidemic behaviour, to the data for deaths from COVID-19, for the UK and Sweden, which we chose because they followed different policies, especially on lockdown; we also fitted it to a global average, to test the model's generality. We have then set out a structural model of the COVID virus behaviour based on evolutionary biology and social household behaviour. We have estimated and tested this by indirect inference, matching its simulated logistic behaviour to that found in the data. We have used these model estimates to assess the effects of the different policies pursued in the two countries. Our basic policy finding is that the general public health policies pursued in Sweden were more effective in reducing deaths than UK public health policies; and that the UK lockdown was no more effective in reducing deaths than the Swedish reliance on voluntary socially aware behaviour, whereas the economic cost of the UK policy was enormously bigger.

NOTE

1. The J-value (cost per life saved by safety measures) used by the US Department of Transportation is between £4 and £10 million per life saved through road safety measures, with the UK value being around £9 million (Thomas, 2018).

REFERENCES

Atkeson, A. (2020), 'What will be the economic impact of COVID-19 in the US? Rough estimates of disease scenarios', *NBER Working Papers*, No. 26867, March 2020.
Batista, M. (2020), 'Estimation of the final size of the coronavirus epidemic by the logistic model', working paper.

Beenstock, M. and X. Dai (2020), 'The natural and unnatural histories of Covid-19 contagion', *Covid Economics: Vetted and Real-Time Papers*, Issue 10, 87–115.

Caldwell, B. (1998), 'Why didn't Hayek review the General Theory?' *History of Political Economy*, **30** (4), 545–69.

Cervia, C., J. Nilsson and Y. Zurbuchem et al. (2020), 'Systemic and mucosal antibody secretion specific to SARS-CoV-2 during mild versus severe COVID-19', *Biorxiv.org*, 23 May, accessed 29 August 2020 at https://www .biorxiv.org/content/10.1101/2020.05.21.108308v1.full.

Cochrane, J. (2020), 'An SIR model with behavior', *Johncochrane.blogspot.com*, 4 May, accessed 29 August 2020 https://johnhcochrane.blogspot.com/2020/ 05/an-sir-model-with-behavior.html.

Dimdore-Miles, O. and D. Miles (2020), 'Assessing the spread of the novel coronavirus in the absence of mass testing', *Covid-19, Vetted and Real Time Papers*, Issue 16, 161–81.

Ellison, M. and A. Scott (2017), '323 years of UK national debt', *Voxeu.org*, 20 October, accessed 29 August 2020 at https://voxeu.org/article/323-years-uk -national-debt.

Golinski, A. and P. Spencer (2020), 'Coronametrics: the UK turns the corner', *University of York Discussion Papers in Economics*, No. 20/04.

Grifoni, A., D. Weiskopf and S. Ramirez et al. (2020), 'Targets of T cell responses to SARS-CoV-2 coronavirus in humans with COVID-19 disease and unexposed individuals', *Cell*, **181**, 1489–501, accessed 29 August 2020 at https://www.cell.com/action/showPdf?pii=S0092-8674%2820%2930610-3-.

Hayek, F.A. (1944), *The Road to Serfdom*, London: Routledge.

Hodge Bank (2020), *Quarterly Economic Bulletin*, July, accessed 29 August 2020 at https://hodgebank.co.uk/wp-content/uploads/2020/07/Hodge-QEB -July-2020.pdf.

Keynes, J.M. (1936), *The General Theory of Employment, Interest and Money*, London: Palgrave Macmillan.

Le, M., D. Meenagh and P. Minford (2019), 'State-dependent pricing turns money into a two-edged sword', *Working Paper E2019-15*, accessed 30 August 2020 at http://carbsecon.com/wp/E2019_15.pdf.

Le, V.P.M., D. Meenagh, P. Minford and M. Wickens (2011), 'How much nominal rigidity is there in the US economy? Testing a New Keynesian DSGE model using indirect inference', *Journal of Economic Dynamics & Control*, **35** (12), 2078–104.

Liu, E., A. Mian and A. Sufi (2019), 'Low interest rates, market power, and productivity growth', Princeton University, accessed 29 August 2020 at https://scholar.princeton.edu/sites/default/files/ernestliu/files/liumiansufi _publicdraft01222019.pdf.

Lourenço, J., R. Paton and M. Ghafari et al. (2020), 'Fundamental principles of epidemic spread highlight the immediate need for large-scale serological surveys to assess the stage or the SARS-CoV-2 epidemic', *Medrxiv.org*, 26 March, accessed 29 August 2020 at https://www.medrxiv.org/content/10 .1101/2020.03.24.20042291v1.full.pdf.

Nesse, R.M., C.T. Bergstrom and P.T. Ellison et al. (2010), 'Making evolutionary biology a basic science for medicine', *Proceedings of the National Academy of Sciences*, **107** (Suppl. 1), 1800–807.

Niemietz, K. (2019), *Socialism: The Failed Idea that Never Dies*, London: Institute of Economic Affairs.

Office for National Statistics (ONS) (2020), *Coronavirus (COVID-19) Infection Survey*, accessed 29 August 2020 at https://www.ons.gov.uk/peoplepopulationandcommunity/healthandsocialcare/conditionsanddiseases/datasets/coronaviruscovid19infectionsurveydata.

Organisation for Economic Co-operation and Development (OECD) (2019), 'Trends in multifactor productivity and capital deepening', accessed 29 August 2020 at https://www.oecd-ilibrary.org/sites/bc0ae2e6-en/index.html?itemId=/content/component/bc0ae2e6-en.

Thomas, P. (2018), 'Calculating the value of human life: safety decision that can be trusted', *Policy Report 25*, April, University of Bristol.

University of Manchester (2020), 'Over 25% of the UK likely to have had COVID-19 already', accessed 29 August 2020 at https://www.manchester.ac.uk/discover/news/over-25-of-the-uk-likely-to-have-had-covid-19-already.

Zitelmann, R. (2018), *The Power of Capitalism*, London: Adam Smith Institute.

6. Reforming monetary policy for a normal future

In previous chapters we reviewed the systematic failure of monetary policy that led to the Great Recession and the regulative overkill we now face in our financial sectors. We can remind ourselves that welfare is maximized by banks when the 'credit friction' (defined as the gap between the rate banks lend at and the return on equity for the firm) is driven to its lowest possible. The reason is that there is no systematic risk on the idiosyncratic firm risks that bedevil banks and create bankruptcy and bad debts; were it possible for these firms to raise equity capital, these risks would be diversified away. Because this is not possible for small firms, banks have a role. However, the more we can lower the extra costs/friction created by this role, the closer we get the cost of finance to the social cost.

It follows that it makes no sense to raise the cost further by bank regulation, unless there is no other way to prevent crises like the financial crisis and the Great Recession. Yet, the whole idea of monetary policy as a stabilizer is to achieve this prevention without regulative distortions. We now go on to discuss how this could be done. We assume we are dealing once again with a normal economy, and that the currently emaciated economy has therefore been restored to health – by the fiscal remedies set out in the last chapter.

Here I draw on recent work (Le, Meenagh and Minford, 2019) that studies the tendencies for price/wage stickiness to vary with inflation. As we saw earlier, when inflation is low and stable, prices and wages get fixed for quite long periods. This is a desirable feature because it also means that inflation varies little and is highly predictable, meaning that the information in the price system is not disturbed by worries about inflation – rather, it reliably just tells us what relative prices are.

Desirable as it is for this reason, price/wage fixity also implies that output is heavily affected by shocks, both demand and supply. The reason is that the movement in prices and wages that would keep output close to the economy's capacity is jammed deliberately; to keep prices and wages fixed at these levels, output and labour must be supplied in line with demand. Supply shocks may drive up prices or wages via costs; these cost increases will then impact demand, and so output and employment. Demand shocks will directly impact on output, and will only affect prices or wages with a lag through induced price/wage responses to excess supply or demand. Indeed, the financial crisis was one such very large demand shock, against which the economy was only weakly protected by monetary policy, as it was only targeting an inflation rate that moved little due to price fixity.

What we also find is that price fixity disappears whenever there is a financial crisis where the zero lower bound (ZLB) occurs. The reason is that at the ZLB monetary policy loses most of its power to stabilize the economy against shocks disturbing output. So, output becomes more volatile, inducing volatility in prices through excess demand. In turn, this price volatility reduces the extent of price stickiness, further boosting price volatility. The result is the worst of all worlds: enough price stickiness to ensure output fluctuates a lot in response to shocks, while not enough to stop prices fluctuating a lot as well. Overall, ZLB episodes unleash large inflation fluctuations, much as we have observed since the financial crisis hit, with inflation being unusually low, close to deflation.

This implies we need some robust way to stop these ZLB episodes in their tracks. As we learnt from Keynes, once monetary policy is rendered powerless by the ZLB (which also occurred in the 1930s), only fiscal policy can stop the episode and return monetary policy its powers. In our recipe for stability we include a key role for fiscal policy to act as a backstop against the ZLB, terminating ZLB episodes rapidly if they occur. This then allows monetary policy full scope to deploy its powers of stabilization.

What we find is that monetary policy now has a twin role: first, to keep prices as stable as possible to encourage long-term price/wage contracts; second, to react quickly and powerfully to the demand shocks that can hit the economy hard in these conditions of wage/price stability.

This is to be contrasted with the situation when existing monetary policies are deployed. In Figure 6.1, we see the shocks identified from the US data by our model of US monetary policy. Analogous work on the UK economy is under development, but, of course, to create true stability we need the US, as the world's largest economy, to pursue these policies itself, so stabilizing the world economy. What we find in our US model simulations – likely to be similar for the UK – is that if interest rate policy targets nominal gross domestic product, together with this fiscal backstop, we maintain long-duration wage and price contracts, so that inflation is very stable, but policy also responds powerfully to demand shocks, shielding the economy from recession.

If we are to keep a stable price level, which seems to be an obviously good idea, even if it is difficult to measure its benefits, then we also need to find a good way to protect the economy against these large demand shocks. The way to do this is for monetary policy to react to movements in the 'output gap', the difference of output from its supply-side equilibrium value. If policy – that is, interest rates – is already reacting to the price level to keep prices stable, then reacting to the output gap as well implies money is reacting to prices and output, or nominal GDP.

What we find is that this nominal GDP targeting works rather well to stabilize the economy, without any need for intrusive regulation. Below are some illustrations of different random-sample histories of the economy under this policy and without it. Also, Table 6.1 shows the main comparison between results with the current policy rule and those with our nominal GDP target as just described. We find that the number of Great Recessions you get on average is only one every century under both rules; however, under the nominal GDP target the variance of inflation falls to one-fifteenth, while the variance of output around its trend falls by a third. The overall welfare cost, a weighted average of the two, falls by two-thirds. The work set out here is for the US economy: we are repeating the analysis for the UK economy in work in progress – we expect the results to be similar.

THE LATEST POLICY ANALYSIS IN THE CONTEXT OF CAPITALIST HISTORY

What we see in recent – that is, post-war – history, is how inflation first got a serious hold on the world economy in response to aggressive Keynesian policies of deficit financing soon after World War II. Governments were determined to achieve full employment via demand stimulus. Not realizing the eventual inflationary impact, they persisted in these policies until inflation was thoroughly embedded in double digits and interest rates had followed it upwards, as savers protected themselves against it.

There followed the period – from around the mid-1970s – of monetarist policies to bring inflation down. These succeeded and, by the 1980s, output had started to recover from the monetary squeeze involved. From the early 1990s, governments began to impose inflation targets on central banks, giving them independence to set policy as needed to achieve them.

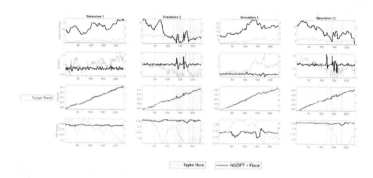

Note: Simulated examples of US monetary rules. Nominal GDP rule shown by black line; existing rule shown by grey lines (with ZLB episodes shown shaded for this rule).
Note: A Taylor Rule is an interest rate rule responding to inflation and output (Taylor, 1999). NGDPT stands for an interest rate rule responding to a nominal GDP target.
Source: Le et al. (2019), Figure 10.

Figure 6.1   Simulation comparison between Taylor Rule and NGDPT with no ZLB

The success of these policies in keeping inflation down created an era of moderate inflation and output stability – giving it the name 'the Great Moderation'.

In response, firms and workers also moderated their price and wage increases, lengthening the duration of price/wage fixity. But, as the work in this chapter reveals, this lengthening made output more responsive to shocks, inflation less responsive. Central banks were lulled into complacency about the effects of looser money and resulting credit creation in the 2000s: there were only mild inflation responses until the commodity price boom beginning after midway through the decade. As central banks started to tighten in response, the ensuing contraction generated bank losses and the resulting financial crisis. As we have seen in the last chapter, central banks, having bred the credit boom, continued to mishandle events – failing to avert the crisis, and then doubling down by introducing draconian new regulations on bank credit, just when this needed to be expanded to create recovery from the crisis.

Table 6.1   Crises and welfare comparison

	Crises/1000 Years (4–6 years long)	var (π)	var (y)[a]	Welfare[b]	Av. NK[c] Weight	Av. NK Weight Price
Taylor Rule[d]	8.10	0.1127	25.2419	0.1755	0.9377	0.9516
NGDPT[e] (no ZLB)	9.72	0.0176	16.8902	0.0598	0.9534	0.9658

Notes:
a. Deviation from target trend.
b. Weighted welfare = 0.9975 × var (π) + 0.0025 × var (y)
c. NK = New Keynesian.
d. A Taylor Rule is an interest rate rule responding to inflation and output (Taylor, 1999).
e. NGDPT = nominal GDP target.
Source: Le et al. (2019), Table 5.

It can be seen across the whole post-war period that both fiscal and monetary policy have been highly active, whether first in pursuing growth, later in curbing inflation, or latterly in creating and responding to the financial crisis. Furthermore, our policy suggestions here remain for active policy: first, for fiscal policy to expand and eliminate the zero interest rate situation, then, this done, for monetary policy to respond strongly to nominal GDP, in order to maintain macro stability.

If one rolls back the story to the end of the nineteenth century, policy was generally not active in any of these ways. Monetary policy was generally disciplined by the gold standard, under which it needed to keep its price in gold fairly constant in the long run. As a result, the rate of growth of money fluctuated around a fairly constant rate. In turn, this meant that inflation was fairly stable around a low average up to World War II. World War I was a dramatic but temporary exception, where commodity prices took off but came back down soon after.

Against this background, the world business cycle was dominated by commodity price fluctuations, mostly very long swings. Le, Meenagh and Minford (2019) set out a model of this cycle behaviour, which they show fits the data rather well (Figure 6.2).

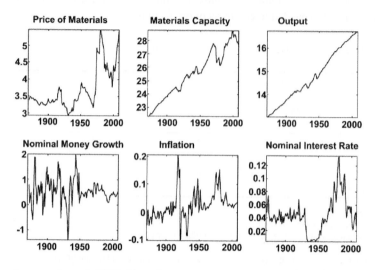

Source: Le et al. (2019), Figure 3.

Figure 6.2   World economy data, 1870–2008

Had these long and moderate fluctuations been all, then the associated monetary policy behaviour would have been rated a general success. Policy behaviour after World War II would also have probably continued in the same vein, avoiding the switch to Keynesian activism from which subsequent events evolved. The big episode that dominated the pre-World War II period was, of course, the Great Depression, which can be seen in Figure 6.2 just before 1939 as one of zero interest rates, falling prices, negative money supply growth and falling output. According to Friedman and Schwarz in *A Monetary History of the United States*, the cause of the Depression was the collapse of US banks and the consequent implosion of money and credit.

The policy reaction after World War II to this cataclysmic interwar event was based on Keynes's analysis in 1936 in *The General Theory of Employment, Interest and Money*. He argued that only fiscal policy could get the world economy back on track, with interest rates at zero rendering monetary policy powerless – a situation we see repeated today. As it happened, it was indeed massive public spending on the war effort that put an end to the interwar zero interest rate environment.

Looking back, we can see that had monetary policy not failed so spectacularly to counteract the 1928–29 contraction, history would undoubtedly have been very different. Not merely would the rise of Hitler probably not have occurred in response to Germany's interwar economic collapse, but that of post-war fiscal activism would also not have happened. Instead, monetary policy could well have continued to have been disciplined by gold, with moderate variation in money supply growth around a moderate constant rate.

As it is, today we find ourselves in a near repeat of the Great Depression, aptly named the Great Recession, and fiscal activism is again needed to dig us out, as we have argued above. Once it has done so, at least a fair period of active monetary policy looks necessary to restore monetary stability. Once it has done so, a more passive policy of simply keeping money and credit growth stable may work well once again, though we would have to see how well that would work in the highly complex world of today, with varying price-/wage-setting behaviour. It could be that the distinction between that and achieving a nominal GDP target through interest rate movements might disappear in practice, with stability in price and money trends and long-term stability in prices and price setting reinforcing one another. Inspection of the simulation figures above suggest this should be the case: our nominal GDP targeting rule is coincident with one in which prices and output, and so money, all follow steady growth trends.

CONCLUSIONS

In this chapter we have reviewed how a reformed monetary rule for setting interest rates, accompanied by a fiscal backstop dedicated to stopping a zero lower bound emerging, could produce a world of both stable prices and stable output, with no need for draconian regulation on banks. We have shown that in our estimated model of the US economy, the dominant one of the Western world, it would work well. It should also work well in the UK and the EU; although we have not yet tested it in models of those economies, other work we have done on these models suggests they are sufficiently similar to respond in the same stabilizing way to a similar monetary reform.

We see our proposed reformed monetary rule as harking back to older rules developed during the gold standard period that stabilized the growth of money and credit around steady trends in prices and output. We think such monetary behaviour would lock in a general tendency towards long-term price contracts, reflecting such a stable price world.

REFERENCES

Friedman, M. and A. Schwarz (1963), *A Monetary History of the United States*, Princeton, NJ: Princeton University Press.

Keynes, J.M. (1936), *The General Theory of Employment, Interest and Money*, London: Palgrave Macmillan.

Le, M., D. Meenagh and P. Minford (2019), 'A long-commodity-cycle model of the world economy over a century and a half – making bricks with little straw', *Energy Economics*, **81** (C) 503–18.

Le, M., D. Meenagh and P. Minford (2019), 'State-dependent pricing turns money into a two-edged sword', *Working Paper E2019-15*, accessed 30 August 2020 at http://carbsecon.com/wp/E2019_15.pdf.

Taylor, J.B. (1999), 'The robustness and efficiency of monetary policy rules as guidelines for interest rate setting by the European Central Bank', *Journal of Monetary Economics*, **43** (3), 655–79.

7. Fiscal rules and the new fiscal programme

Boris Johnson's Conservative government, having succeeded in getting Brexit done, will be faced with a quite new situation once the coronavirus lockdown is over – a situation we discussed at some length in Chapter 5. Fiscal policy, as we argued in the last chapter, needs to take brutal advantage of the negative real interest rates on government borrowing to reform/bring down taxes and spend on necessary infrastructure. In the process, it will drive up interest rates and restore power to monetary policy, currently a busted flush due to serial central bank mistakes since the beginning of the millennium. Hence, we need a period where fiscal policy is highly expansionary, to shift the world balance back towards a savings shortage and drive up rates. Fortunately, this is the approach both of Donald Trump and Boris Johnson, so both the US and the UK are now embarking on sizeable deficits, with 'austerity' well buried. Unfortunately, the EU is gripped by German fiscal orthodoxy – macroeconomics is barely understood by German politicians, and where they do get some glimmering, is regarded as the work of the devil, and specially designed to transfer German money to foreigners. So, the chances of fiscal expansion in the EU are poor at present. In Japan too, policy is inert – monetary policy powerless as here and fiscal policy hamstrung by a huge public debt/gross domestic product (GDP) ratio of 245%. As it is almost entirely domestically held by Japanese households happy to hold money and saving heavily due to ageing, this is not a problem, but the Abe government saw it as one.

Notice that when we wound up our discussion of the fiscal outcomes from the coronavirus crisis, we saw that because interest rate costs of the fiscal packages deployed were so low, the necessary rise in taxes to pay for it were easily manageable. There would be no need for a period of 'austerity' to pay off debts that in market value would be quite low relative to GDP. It follows that old short-term rules devised to balance budget deficits and enforce such repayment need reconsideration. It is to be hoped that the experience of responding to the virus lockdown crisis will have refreshed people's minds on the working mechanics of fiscal policy; it should have demonstrated the massive power of sovereign governments to borrow and create money as needed to carry out necessary social programmes, whether in tax or spending reform. In this chapter we propose alternative long-term rules concerned with fiscal solvency and use them to propose new creative approaches to fiscal policy that will allow serious reforms of our tax and spending systems.

So, as so often, the world now depends on the Anglo-Saxons: this time pulling it out of the zero interest world with fiscal activism, so that monetary policy can rise from the ashes. To begin this process, they will need new fiscal rules, appropriate for the long term, in place of the short-termist rules currently in operation, focused on limiting either the current budget deficit or the public sector borrowing requirement (PSBR), or both. What these long-term rules should be, we turn to next.

ASSESSING THE PROJECTED GOVERNMENT BALANCE SHEET: THE METHODS THAT SHOULD BE USED

Assessing whether fiscal policy is responsible or not, a variety of fiscal rules have been proposed. Currently, the prevailing rule is that either the current budget deficit or the PSBR should be eliminated over the next few years and even pushed into surplus. Another proposal has been that the current budget should be balanced, allowing capital spending to be financed by borrowing. This would allow infrastructure spending to go ahead unhindered. However, a little thought shows that these rules are quite superficial. We need instead to project the public balance sheet we will end up with after following projected policies. The state of this balance sheet – notably, the level of projected debt at market value – determines whether the government will need to raise new taxes in the future. This being politically difficult at the best of times, it acts as a key constraint on what the government can afford to do.

The future projected balance sheet (+ assets; – liabilities) for 2027 is shown in Box 7.1.

BOX 7.1   FUTURE PROJECTED BALANCE SHEET FOR 2027

Projected present value (PV) of outstanding bonds (= PV of future bond interest and capital payments) – bonds' market value (note, this takes account of capital value changes due to changing interest rates).

PV of future spending including debt interest: – future spend.

PV of future tax revenue at current rates: + future tax revenue.

= Projected negative balance to be offset by new future taxes: future spend) – future tax revenue = projected fiscal gap.

Required extra taxes = fiscal gap × interest rate.

Notice that infrastructure is not entered at cost or indeed at all; its effects come in indirectly through promising to generate growth and so tax revenue with current taxes. The key element in the balance sheet is the projected market value of debt as a percentage of GDP. Provided this is kept below some safe percentage – usually thought of as around 60% there will be no threat of needing to raise new taxes. The government should be able to pay for debt interest and continuing normal spending (on both capital and current needs) from normal existing tax revenue.

BUDGETING FOR BREXIT: EVALUATING FOUR BUDGETARY PROGRAMMES

To illustrate these principles, we look at four different fiscal scenarios in the UK, projecting detailed figures for each scenario, based on our Cardiff models of the UK. For this purpose, we ignore the COVID crisis recession, and what we argued earlier would be a V-shaped recovery. Also, we ignore the interest cost of the COVID crisis fiscal deficits, which, owing to the extremely low interest rate, implies only a small burden on the taxpayer; our most recent published forecasts (in the Hodge Bank *Quarterly Economic Bulletin*, July 2020) show how we think this will evolve. Hence, in what follows, our projections are all pre-COVID crisis.

Comparing the Potential Post-Brexit Outlooks

What we do next is to set out four potential outlooks post-Brexit in some detail:

1. The post-Brexit baseline: this assumes no change in policy from where we are now, other than delivering the EU deal on Brexit, and

    then moving to free trade agreements (FTAs) with both the EU and the rest of the world, on assumptions set out in earlier chapters.

2. The Conservative 2019 election manifesto: here we take the manifesto's projections for fiscal policy literally and project their effects on growth, the public finances, inflation and interest rates, adding them to the baseline, where we assume the same Brexit policies are carried out.

3. The Labour 2019 election manifesto: here we take the Labour programme of radical change in economic policies and project their general effects on the economy and the public finances. Given the strong protestations of intent from Labour's leaders, we take the programme as a serious set of planned policies to be carried out as planned by a future Labour government. In fact, the newly elected leader, Sir Keir Starmer, seems to be moving away from this programme, for good.

4. Fiscal Fund Plus: here we consider the post-election follow-up policies that build on the supply-side reform possibilities opened up by Brexit and that we would advocate. We note the potential in the baseline public finance projections (we call this the Fiscal Fund) for a bold programme of tax cuts, plus the need to raise interest rates to escape from the zero lower bound (ZLB), in a way we discussed in the chapter on fiscal and monetary policy. Hence, our title for this programme 'Fiscal Fund Plus'.

THE POST-BREXIT BASELINE AND THE EFFECTS OF BREXIT

In the baseline post-Brexit forecast shown in Table 7.1 we make assumptions about the Brexit effects as follows. The long-run gains, as estimated from our research, come from four main sources (Meenagh and Minford, 2020; Minford, 2020):

- moving to free trade with non-EU countries that currently face high EU protection in goods trade;
- substituting UK-based regulation for EU-based Single Market regulation;
- ending the large subsidy that the 'four freedoms' forces the UK to give to EU unskilled immigrants;
- ending our budget contribution to the EU.

In total, these four elements, according to research in Cardiff, create a rise in GDP in the long term over the next decade and a half of about 7%, which is equivalent to an average rise in the growth rate of around 0.5% p.a. If we leave with no deal, that is, under World Trade Organization (WTO) rules with piecemeal side-agreements, we gain on top of this about £500 billion in one-off present value terms from extra tariff revenues at the expense of the EU.

At the heart of our estimates lie models that assume a world of tough long-run competition in which industries can only survive by matching the competitive norm. By contrast, the consensus among trade theorists is that competing firms have significant monopoly power due to their unique brands; this theory is known as 'gravity' modelling, in which natural monopoly power arises simply from size and proximity to consumers. On this view, cutting into rival markets is hard, and this fact also protects their own market position. Along with this view goes an interventionist theory of regulation: that 'rights' can be awarded to 'stakeholders' at the expense of monopolist firms, with little damage to their competitive position. Along with it too goes the view that productivity growth occurs automatically as a result of growing trade, itself a product of proximity.

In our research we find a very different world: a world in which lagging firms can be largely destroyed, with examples like Nokia and BlackBerry coming to mind. We see the role of supply chains as squeezing out uncompetitive intermediate producers who do not devote enough effort to raising productivity via innovation. In this world, business regulation can easily damage competitiveness. This is particularly true of labour market regulation, for which we have good estimates of the damage based on UK experience (see Chapter 2 in Minford et al., 2015).

In our Cardiff World Trade Model, we embed these assumptions and test their predictions against the facts of UK trade. We also set up a rival 'gravity model' as set out in Chapter 2. We test these models by indirect inference against the UK facts (Minford and Xu, 2018; for details see the appendix to chapter 2 of this book). This test is based on simulating each model many times to generate a full range of counterfactual histories due to randomly chosen re-runs of historical shocks; we then ask how probable the actual UK history would have been if the model were correct. What we find is that the gravity model is highly improbable, well below a 5% minimum threshold of rejection, whereas the Cardiff model is fairly probable, comfortably above this rejection level.

The implications of the Cardiff models for Brexit are radical. Brexit will usher in a world in which, for the first time in our post-war history,

Table 7.1   Summary of the post-Brexit baseline forecast

	2018	2019	2020	2021	2022	2023	2024	2025	2026	2027	2028	2029	2030
GDP growth[a]	1.4	1.5	1.9	1.9	2.1	2.1	2.0	2.0	2.0	2.0	2.1	2.1	2.0
Inflation CPI[b]	2.5	1.9	2.1	2.0	2.0	2.0	2.0	2.0	2.0	2.0	2.0	2.0	2.0
Wage growth	3.1	3.6	3.1	3.1	3.1	3.2	3.2	3.3	3.3	3.3	3.4	3.3	3.2
Unemployment (million)[c]	0.9	0.9	0.8	0.7	0.7	0.6	0.6	0.6	0.6	0.6	0.6	0.6	0.6
Exchange rate[d]	78.6	80.1	80.7	80.6	80.5	80.4	80.3	80.2	80.1	79.9	79.8	79.7	79.5
Three-month interest rate	0.7	0.9	4.7	4.2	3.3	3.0	2.5	2.3	2.1	2.0	2.0	2.0	2.0
Five-year interest rate	1.0	1.0	1.3	2.4	3.3	3.4	3.3	2.6	2.4	2.2	2.0	2.0	2.0
Current balance (£ billion)	−81.3	−86.5	−41.3	−3.14	−23.3	−15.0	−11.9	−11.3	−14.5	−9.4	−59.	−0.1	3.0
PSBR[e] (£ billion)	40.8	37.8	20.7	8.2	3.9	0.5	−3.2	−5.4	−17.4	−30.2	−45.1	−58.6	−71.9

Notes:
a. Expenditure estimate at factor cost.
b. Consumer price index.
c UK wholly unemployed excluding school leavers (new basis).
d. Sterling effective exchange rate, Bank of England Index (2005 = 100).
e. Public sector borrowing requirement.
Source: Meenagh and Minford (2020); Minford (2020); other author calculations.

the UK market will be entirely dominated by world competition, finally admitted by abandoning EU protection of farming and manufacturing. UK firms and farms will have to be competitive with the best the world has to offer; plainly, this will lower prices to the consumer and raise UK productivity. Notice that because UK service sectors have never had EU protection, not much changes for them in terms of necessary world competitiveness. To ensure this competitiveness UK regulations will have to be business friendly; utterly gone will be the idea that there is some 'free lunch' of 'rights' to be exacted from the business community for the benefit of particular constituencies.

What then of the position of EU firms in these UK markets? It will have fundamentally changed. Instead of being able to sell food and manufactures to UK consumers at inflated prices, owing to the lack of world competition, they will have to sell here at world prices, some 20% lower if EU protection is entirely removed. Were they not to match these prices they would simply be pushed out of the UK market, to sell nothing at all.

It needs to be understood just how large a change this is for EU exporters to the UK. The UK constitutes about a quarter of the whole EU consumer market. If prices fall by a fifth, their margins on a quarter of their sales may well be entirely wiped out.

But matters do not end there. If there is no UK–EU FTA, then both sides must levy tariffs on the other to comply with WTO rules, otherwise they must abolish their tariffs on everyone. But the EU will not because it is protectionist; the UK will not, because it wants to use its tariffs as leverage in FTAs with other countries.

UK tariff revenues from EU exports are estimated at £13 billion a year. But notice that these cannot be passed on to UK consumers after Brexit and UK FTAs around the world. EU exporters must match those world prices in the UK market, so bang goes another £13 billion bite into their margins.

Can the EU recoup these losses by their tariffs on UK exporters? This revenue is estimated at £5 billion a year. But notice these UK exporters now can sell their output at world prices at home; they will sell abroad at the same prices – arbitrage will force that. Abroad now includes the EU. The EU tariffs will therefore be passed on to EU consumers. This will not damage their sales compared with pre-Brexit, because their prices will still be competitive; pre-Brexit they were equal to world prices plus EU protection (tariffs plus non-tariff barriers), post-Brexit equal to home/ world prices plus tariffs (only tariffs, as there cannot be non-tariff barriers with the UK, standards being identical).

FISCAL ARITHMETIC AND OPPORTUNITIES IN THE POST-BREXIT ECONOMY

Projecting the Effects of the Conservative 2019 Election Manifesto

When we turn to the two main party manifestos, we find highly contrasting plans. First, the Conservatives adhered to the latest fiscal rules, in which the current budget should be in surplus in the near future, while extra money may be borrowed to pay for capital investment. Given that they place a priority on enhancing various spending flows, notably on the National Health Service, they actually cancelled the planned cut in corporation tax to 17% to pay for these under the current budget. The only tax cut they put forward is a rise in the National Insurance contribution threshold by workers.

When one adds up all these changes, the Conservatives would spend approximately an extra £25 billion a year, borrowing to finance the £20 billion of capital spending in this. The rest involves a net rise in taxes to pay for it. If, as we assume is reasonable, we assess the supply-side effect of infrastructure spending on a par with that of tax cuts to the same value, then the programme raises growth by 0.2% p.a. over the baseline.

Because fiscal expansion is so limited, interest rates continue much as in the baseline, rising slowly to around 3% by the mid-2020s. The PSBR projection is small and turns negative in the late-2020s. For a summary and fiscal projection under the Conservative manifesto, see Tables 7.2 and 7.3. The future projected balance sheet for 2027 under the Conservative manifesto is shown in Box 7.2.

BOX 7.2   BALANCE SHEET BY 2027 UNDER CONSERVATIVE MANIFESTO

Debt (net of capital gain): no change on post-Brexit baseline.

Debt/GDP ratio 2027: 62.6%.

Future spending p.a. including debt interest = 40% of GDP.

Effect on future tax revenues of induced growth: +3%. Giving annual revenues p.a. = 40% of GDP.

Projected present value (PV) of future tax revenues minus future spending including debt interest, % of GDP = $(1/0.05) \times (41 - 40) =$ 0% of GDP.

Fiscal requirement 2027, % of GDP = PV of future net revenues = 0% of GDP.

Required tax rise = fiscal gap times interest rate = $0 \times 0.05 = 0\%$ of GDP.

What we see from these plans is that they leave the baseline largely untouched in terms of fiscal outcomes. They are cautious in the extreme. We discuss below under our 'Fiscal Fund Plus' a much bolder use of the post-Brexit fiscal possibilities.

Projecting the Effects of the Labour 2019 Election Manifesto

For a summary and fiscal projection under the Labour manifesto, see Table 7.4. If, as we will argue below, a Fiscal Fund Plus programme of heavier future spending/tax cuts is safe, would it not then be equally safe for Labour to go ahead with its much bigger planned programme of higher spending?

If the economy were to remain robust and continue to grow as projected under the Labour programme, then the mere fact of it borrowing large amounts could potentially be absorbed safely according to the arguments we have deployed. Thus, below we have projected the Fiscal Fund Plus addition to the PSBR compared with the no-change baseline at a cumulative £500 billion by 2027. Were Labour to do the same, with the same accompanying policies, there would be no problem.

The difficulties with the Labour programme arise from two damaging elements. The first and most problematic is that the 'accompanying policies' are highly damaging to growth, via effects on the economy's supply side. Labour has said it will raise income tax rates on 'the rich'; these will damage growth for just the same reasons we will argue that Fiscal Fund Plus tax cuts would raise growth. In fact, these higher rate tax rates raise little if any money, so that income tax rates at large (or similar taxes on consumption) will need to rise. Also, Labour has suggested it will not pay full market value to shareholders and landlords whose property it nationalizes (nationalization has now been extended to BT OpenReach in a bid to spread free broadband); such a wealth tax would undermine the confidence of investors and act like other taxes in lowering growth.

Table 7.2   *Summary table for Conservative manifesto*

	2018	2019	2020	2021	2022	2023	2024	2025	2026	2027	2028	2029	2030
GDP growth[a]	1.4	1.5	2.2	2.5	2.1	2.1	2.2	2.2	2.2	2.3	2.3	2.3	2.3
Inflation CPI[b]	2.5	2.0	2.1	2.0	2.0	2.0	2.0	2.0	2.0	2.0	2.0	2.0	2.0
Wage growth	3.1	3.7	3.0	3.2	3.3	3.2	3.2	3.3	3.3	3.3	3.4	3.3	3.2
Unemployment (million)[c]	0.9	0.9	0.8	0.7	0.7	0.6	0.6	0.6	0.6	0.6	0.6	0.6	0.6
Exchange rate[d]	78.6	80.2	80.6	80.6	80.6	80.4	80.2	80.0	79.9	79.8	79.7	79.6	79.5
Three-month interest rate	0.7	0.9	1.1	1.8	2.5	3.2	3.1	2.6	2.3	2.1	2.1	2.1	2.1
Five-year interest rate	1.0	1.0	1.3	2.4	3.3	3.4	3.3	2.6	2.4	2.2	2.0	2.0	2.0
Current balance (£ billion)	−81.3	−86.6	−41.3	−31.3	−23.2	−14.9	−11.8	−11.1	−14.3	−9.2	−5.8	0.1	3.1
PSBR[e] (£ billion)	40.8	37.6	30.0	16.4	12.4	9.0	5.0	2.2	−9.9	−25.7	−38.9	−53.0	−67.3

Notes:
a. Expenditure estimate at factor cost.
b. Consumer price index.
c   UK wholly unemployed excluding school leavers (new basis).
d. Sterling effective exchange rate, Bank of England Index (2005 = 100).
e. Public sector borrowing requirement.
Source: Meenagh and Minford (2020); Minford (2020); other author calculations.

Table 7.3   *Fiscal projection for Conservative manifesto (£ billion, current prices)*

	Brexit PSBR	Debt	GDP (market price)	Debt/GDP %
2018	41.4	1559	2127	73.3
2019	37.4	1716	2215	77.5
2020	30	1746	2310	75.6
2021	16	1762	2401	73.4
2022	12	1774	2506	70.7
2023	9	1783	2614	65.4
2024	5	1788	2726	65.6
2025	2	1790	2842	63.0
2026	−10	1780	2963	60.1
2027	−45	1936	3092	62.6

Source: Meenagh and Minford (2020); Minford (2020); other author calculations.

On the Brexit side of policy, Labour would negotiate effectively not to have Brexit – either with its proposed deal to stay in the EU in all but name or with its referendum alternative of straight Remain. This would imply a supply-side hit to the economy compared with our post-Brexit projection. This is without counting the effects of more prolonged uncertainty on the economy.

Then there is the proposal for a four-day week, which again will reduce output by about a fifth (the equivalent of a 20% tax on employment) unless the government pays workers an overtime subsidy, requiring yet more income taxes. On top of it all, Labour proposes to bring back the union laws abolished by Margaret Thatcher, returning our industrial relations to 1970s chaos; we have not added in the effects of this, which on its own would cause massive supply-side damage.

There is much else in the fine print of Labour's programme that openly plans to replace the 'capitalist' economy we have with one of overwhelming state ownership and direction. This explicit model of state planning has been widely experimented with in other countries: Russia, Cuba, Venezuela are three prominent examples. The results have obviously been disastrous.

So, Labour's programme threatens growth directly. That is its fundamental flaw. As for its borrowing plans, it appears to plan to borrow massively for an infrastructure programme of about £100 billion a year,

Table 7.4   Summary table for Labour manifesto

	2018	2019	2020	2021	2022	2023	2024	2025	2026	2027	2028	2029	2030
GDP growth[a]	1.4	1.5	-0.2	-0.2	-0.1	0.0	-0.1	-0.2	0.0	-0.2	0.2	0.1	0.1
Inflation CPI[b]	2.5	1.9	4.9	5.2	5.2	4.8	5.1	4.9	4.9	4.8	4.7	4.7	4.7
Wage growth	3.1	3.6	3.8	5.8	6.3	6.0	6.3	6.1	6.2	6.1	6.0	6.1	6.0
Unemployment (million)[c]	0.9	1.0	1.0	1.3	1.5	1.9	2.3	2.8	3.4	4.1	5.1	6.2	7.5
Exchange rate[d]	78.6	80.1	69.6	66.8	64.5	62.5	60.4	58.6	57.0	55.5	54.0	52.7	51.4
Three-month interest rate	0.7	0.9	4.9	5.2	4.6	4.8	4.7	4.7	4.7	4.9	4.9	4.9	4.9
Five-year interest rate	1.0	1.0	5.0	5.0	5.1	4.9	4.9	4.7	4.8	4.8	4.8	4.8	4.8
Current balance (£ billion)	-81.3	-86.6	-12.2	-1.1	4.1	8.9	12.0	14.7	12.8	19.4	23.6	27.8	31.6
PSBR[e] (£ billion)	40.8	47.4	59.5	70.5	92.8	121.7	154.5	199.2	234.0	275.9	319.3	369.5	424.8

Notes:
a. Expenditure estimate at factor cost.
b. Consumer price index.
c   UK wholly unemployed excluding school leavers (new basis).
d. Sterling effective exchange rate, Bank of England Index (2005 = 100).
e. Public sector borrowing requirement.
Source: Meenagh and Minford (2020); Minford (2020); other author calculations.

about £55 billion above the baseline. Cumulatively, by 2027, this would come to an extra £440 billion on the baseline. On non-infrastructure spending it plans to fund the extra with the tax rises just mentioned, with their consequential damage to growth.

The Labour programme's effect on growth also seriously undermines projected ongoing tax revenue from 2027, causing a need for yet more new taxes, which must undermine confidence in its ability to remain solvent.

But in the short run it should remove the ZLB issue rapidly. Sterling would collapse, sending inflation up sharply and causing a large outflow from the gilts market, with fears of future UK government insolvency from the fall in future revenues. Long-term and short-term interest rates would rise sharply. However, monetary policy would be unable to stimulate the economy by lowering rates because of the effects on inflation. So, this would be an expensive 'cure' of the ZLB problem, ushering in a monetary policy as fettered as before but in a different way.

The implications of this rapid rise in interest rates is radical. It means that Labour will enjoy a quick fall in the capital value of outstanding debt when it comes in, but that it will then pay higher interest rates for all its new debt. This is what we project for the long-term balance sheet, in Box 7.3.

BOX 7.3 THE LONG-RUN LABOUR PUBLIC SECTOR BALANCE SHEET – FISCAL CHANGES UNDER LABOUR PLANS

Extra spending on infrastructure to be borrowed: £55 billion p.a.

Extra income taxes to pay for other spending: c. £80 billion p.a. (5% rise in top income tax rate and 7% rise in corporation tax rate to pay for this) – effect on output by 2027 = –6%, on top of fall of 7% due to abandoning Brexit.

Add effect of 32-hour working week (an effective employer tax of 20%), –10%, total effect on output –23%.

Add back the positive effect of the higher infrastructure spend on growth (assume equivalent of tax cut to same value p.a. viz. c. 10%); gives offsetting gain to growth of +5%.

Net total effect on output = –17% (–2.1% p.a. off growth).

Note that for this projection we make the most favourable possible assumptions about its manifesto commitments – namely, that the taxes it proposes to raise (the 'basic top' income tax rate from 40% to 45%; and the corporation tax rate from 19% to 26%) are sufficient in their yield to fund its non-infrastructure commitments to spend more, which are set at £80 billion per year. The key effects projected are on GDP, from these tax rises and the 32-hour week (equivalent to an employer tax rise of 20%); of course, these in turn lower the revenues from existing taxes in general. In the Liverpool model, used to estimate the effects of the Thatcher tax changes in the 1980s, a 2% rise in the income tax rate produces a 1% fall in output long term.

The future projected balance sheet for 2027 under the Labour manifesto is shown in Box 7.4.

BOX 7.4   BALANCE SHEET BY 2027 UNDER LABOUR MANIFESTO

Debt (net of capital gain in 2020 of 490): +1500 (£ billion).

GDP by 2027: –17% (compared with post-Brexit baseline).

Debt/GDP ratio 2027: 90%.

Future spending including debt interest, % of GDP: 53%.

Effect on future tax revenues of lower growth : –22% (compared with post-Brexit baseline).

Future tax revenues, % of GDP = 45 (post-tax rises) × 0.93 (fall of revenue/GDP due to lower growth) = 42%.

Fiscal gap (% of GDP): project present value (PV) of net revenue = $(1/0.05) \times -9) = -180\%$.

Required future tax rise = $180 \times 0.05 = 9\%$ of GDP.

What we see here is a long-term balance sheet by 2027 in which debt market value will reach around 90% of GDP, even after initial capital gains from higher interest rates and substantially more inflation-boosting nominal GDP. While higher spending that is continuing will be balanced by higher taxation, those higher taxes will be damaging future growth and bringing down general tax revenues. To pay higher debt interest payments and fund ongoing spending, taxes will need to be raised again substantially, by 9% of GDP, from 2027; the fiscal gap in present value will be 180% of GDP. This is a recipe for insolvency, as taxpayers will be extremely hostile to yet higher tax demands, having already paid up for large tax rises in the 2020s.

BUDGETING AFTER BREXIT – FISCAL SCOPE IN THE BASELINE: THE FISCAL FUND PLUS PROGRAMME

There is another possible programme of post-Brexit policy, which builds on the caution of the Conservative manifesto to pursue a more ambitious programme of tax cuts and spending, fully warranted by the Fiscal Fund and the need to push interest rates up out of the ZLB: Fiscal Fund Plus. Here we show the economic projections generally under this Fiscal Fund Plus programme. Highlights are that interest rates rise to 5% by the early 2020s, that inflation rises a little to the 2–3% range and the economy grows at close to 3% (Table 7.5).

In Table 7.6 we show the updated Cardiff macro group calculations for projected government borrowing post-Brexit, in the light of our latest forecasts. We build in assumptions about the government's projected additional post-Brexit spending plans, which we have called the 'Fiscal Fund'.

Our latest updated budget for Brexit on the current post-Brexit forecast shows substantial scope for cuts in taxes and additional spending on infrastructure and vital public services. The projection in Table 7.6 shows that additional measures costing £25 billion a year from 2020 and an extra £65 billion a year from 2025 are consistent with bringing public debt down to around 60% of GDP by 2027. This debt is counted free of any bank monetary operations, on the assumption that the Bank of England unwinds all its operations in public debt, reversing quantitative easing (QE); this is in line with the assumption that monetary policy would be normalized by then. This implies that all public debt is held outside the public sector itself – at present about a third is held by the bank and so is not public sector debt at all in theory.

The key point, however, at present is to note the overwhelming need, explained above, for fiscal policy to drive up interest rates. This could well call for a lot more borrowing than is pencilled into the table; we cannot know how much is needed until we see how interest rates respond.

Table 7.5　　Summary table for Fiscal Fund Plus

	2018	2019	2020	2021	2022	2023	2024	2025	2026	2027	2028	2029	2030
GDP growth[a]	1.4	1.5	2.7	3.1	3.2	3.1	3.0	3.0	3.0	3.1	3.1	3.1	3.3
Inflation CPI[b]	2.5	2.0	2.1	2.1	2.1	2.0	2.0	2.1	2.1	2.1	2.0	2.0	2.1
Wage growth	3.1	3.6	3.5	3.7	3.7	3.8	3.8	3.9	3.9	3.8	3.9	3.8	3.8
Unemployment (million)[c]	0.9	0.9	0.8	0.7	0.7	0.6	0.6	0.6	0.6	0.6	0.6	0.6	0.6
Exchange rate[d]	78.6	80.1	80.6	80.5	80.4	80.3	80.3	80.2	80.1	80.1	80.0	79.9	79.9
Three-month interest rate	0.7	0.9	3.7	4.6	5.0	5.1	5.0	5.0	5.0	5.0	5.0	5.0	5.0
Five-year interest rate	1.0	1.0	4.3	4.9	5.3	5.3	5.1	5.0	5.0	5.0	5.0	5.0	5.0
Current balance (£ billion)	-81.3	-84.1	-35.3	-26.6	-22.3	-13.2	-9.8	-8.9	-11.9	-5.9	-1.7	4.3	7.6
PSBR[e] (£ billion)	40.8	40.6	52.4	40.9	39.8	39.9	42.4	50.9	46.9	40.6	35.0	29.0	19.9

Notes:
a. Expenditure estimate at factor cost.
b. Consumer price index.
c　UK wholly unemployed excluding school leavers (new basis).
d. Sterling effective exchange rate, Bank of England Index (2005 = 100).
e. Public sector borrowing requirement.
Source:　Meenagh and Minford (2020); Minford (2020); other author calculations.

Table 7.6   *The path of public borrowing and debt with the post-Brexit Fiscal Fund (£ billion, current prices)*

	Brexit PSBR	+Fiscal Fund	Debt	GDP (market price)	Debt/GDP %
2018	41.4		1559	2127	73.3
2019	37.4		1716	2215	77.5
2020	20.4	+25	1761	2310	76.2
2021	7.0	+25	1793	2410	74.4
2022	3.0	+25	1821	2514	72.4
2023	−10.0	+25	1836	2630	69.8
2024	−15.5	+25	1846	2753	67.0
2025	−25.0	+65	1885	2891	65.2
2026	−35.0	+65	1916	3035	63.1
2027	−45.0	+65	1936	3187	60.7

Note: Public sector net debt (excluding public sector banks) estimated at £1646 billion at end 2017–18 FY (in September 2017 £1638 billion; source: Office for National Statistics).
Source: Meenagh and Minford (2020); Minford (2020); other author calculations.

But to those who fear the government risks insolvency by being so aggressive in fiscal policy, we make two points. First, in the current marketplace, government bond issues are being priced at extremely low interest rates (around 0.4% p.a. currently) because they are seen uniquely as entirely safe – the UK government has never defaulted and is backed by UK taxpayers, law-abiding people/firms who always pay up. Second, suppose the government, for example, issues £220 billion of debt over the coming decade as we assume and it does so at current rates (R) of around 0.4%. Then suppose, in 2027, interest rates have risen to 5%. Make the simple assumption purely for ease of illustration that all this debt is perpetuities paying an annual coupon, whose price is therefore coupon/R. Then the £220 billion issue turns out in 2027 to be worth only £18 billion; the government makes a substantial capital gain, which plainly protects its solvency in a strong way. Effectively, it will only have really borrowed £18 billion, and its market value of debt/GDP ratio in 2027 would be correspondingly reduced.

Most commentators, including the Office for Budget Responsibility (OBR), the Institute for Fiscal Studies (IFS), most macro forecasters, and even it would seem the Treasury itself, have not caught up with these key facts of the macro situation, and hence are giving advice that is quite outdated. As Lord Keynes once said: 'If the facts change, I change my mind; what do you do?'

The Effects of Using the Post-Brexit Fiscal Fund

Matters do not end there. The Fiscal Fund will have dynamic effects on the UK economy by cutting taxes and boosting growth-friendly infra-structure. Our arithmetic above computes the debt evolution on the basis of £65 billion p.a. fiscal expansion by 2025, on the assumption that solvency concerns drive debt to a 'safe' 60% of GDP by 2027. As we have said, fiscal policy should be more aggressive than this in order to drive up interest rates to reasonable levels at which monetary policy bites again. Such rates might be around 5% and require a lot more borrowing than we have assumed in our 'safe' arithmetic; indeed, to drive UK rates up, if world rates remain mired around 2–3%, the UK has to look more risky and the pound be forced to strengthen by seriously aggressive borrowing. For illustrative purposes we will assume the extra borrowing reaches £100 billion pa by 2025 – we will call this 'Fiscal Fund Plus'.

This would make possible various tax cuts which could boost the UK's competitiveness. Here is the current cost of such tax cuts – a 1% rate cut in:

- corporation tax would cost £3.2 billion by 2025;
- the standard rate of income tax £5.6 billion;
- the top rate of income tax £1.5 billion;
- the very top ('additional') rate £0.2 billion.

So, a cocktail of pro-entrepreneur tax cuts and spending changes worth £100 billion could be:

- cut corporation tax by 10%: £32 billion;
- abolish the very top additional 5% rate: £1 billion;
- cut the top rate of income tax to 30%: £15 billion;
- cut the standard rate of income tax by 5%: £28 billion.

This would give a total of £76 billion, representing a weighted average tax cut across all income of about 15%, leaving £24 billion extra (about 1% of GDP) for spending on public services and infrastructure. According to the Liverpool supply-side model of the UK, every 2% off the average tax rate gains 1% on GDP in the long run by making the labour market more competitive. The second-round effects of Brexit through the Fiscal Fund

Plus would therefore boost the economy by a further 7% over the decade from 2020 – or another 0.7% pa on growth from 2020 to 2030. How should we evaluate the effects of the remaining £24 billion extra spend on public services? We know that these also boost growth by raising private productivity, we assume by the same as the same amount in tax cuts. This would add another 0.23% p.a. to the growth rate. On this basis we could project the whole post-Brexit programme from the new Fund could boost growth from 2025 by some 1% p.a.

In the tables we projected the programme before counting the extra spending/tax cuts made necessary by the crisis with the ZLB. We suggested that this could push the Fiscal Fund up to £100 billion by 2025 – the Fiscal Fund Plus. We assume this extra would come in gradually, reaching a further £35 billion by 2025. The idea of these higher deficits is to stimulate the economy and so raise interest rates to normal rates close to 5%. The amount needed would be kept under review in the light of the interest rate situation. But so stubborn is the ZLB proving, these figures look a likely projection as of now.

They would raise the debt/GDP ratio to 67% of GDP by 2027 – before taking account of the capital gain coming from higher interest rates. This would put off the date at which the safe 60% debt ratio would be reached to 2031, the end of the decade. However, this calculation does not take account of the capital gain we explained earlier, produced by the rise in long-term interest rates. Given that UK public debt has an average life of 16 years, a rise of rates to 5% from 1.5% when issued over the next few years (assumed to be above the current 1%) would bring in a capital gain, through lowering the value of debt, of about £400 billion. This would imply that the safe debt/GDP ratio would be reached comfortably earlier than 2027 even with the Fiscal Fund Plus programme. In fact, the projected date is around 2024.

This illustrates perfectly how a bold fiscal strategy designed to generate supply-side improvements and stimulate interest rates up to normal rates is entirely feasible and safe in current circumstances. Our projection of the fiscal gap by 2027 is –20% of GDP in present value, implying that a tax cut of 1% of GDP is possible.

The balance sheet by 2027 under Fiscal Fund Plus is shown in Box 7.5 and the terminal public sector balance sheet for each forecast, values projected 2027, is shown in Table 7.7. Figures 7.1–7.4 summarize the different scenarios that have been discussed throughout the chapter.

Table 7.7   *Terminal public sector balance sheets for each forecast*
                    – values projected 2027

	Baseline	Conservative	Labour	Reform
Debt/GDP ratio (%)	50.7	62.6	90	55
Ongoing 2027 spending and revenue:				
Govt. spending (incl. debt interest)/GDP (%)	40	40	53	40
Ongoing tax revenue/GDP (%)	40	40	42	41
Required future tax rise/GDP (%)	0	0	11	−1

Note: Debt valued after effect of long-term interest rates on capital value.
Source: Meenagh and Minford (2020); Minford (2020); other author calculations.

BOX 7.5   BALANCE SHEET BY 2027 UNDER FISCAL FUND PLUS

Debt (net of capital gain): (compared with post-Brexit no-Fiscal Fund baseline)

Debt (market value)/GDP ratio 2027: 55%.

Future spending p.a. including debt interest = 40% of GDP.

Effect on future tax revenues of Fiscal Fund-induced growth: +10%. Giving annual revenues p.a. = 41% of GDP.

Projected present value (PV) of future tax revenues minus future spending including debt interest, % of GDP = $(1/.05) \times (41{-}40) = 20\%$ of GDP.

Fiscal requirement 2027, % of GDP = PV of future net revenues = $-20\% = -20\%$ of GDP.

Required tax rise = fiscal gap times interest rate = $-20 \times 0.05 = -1\%$ of GDP.

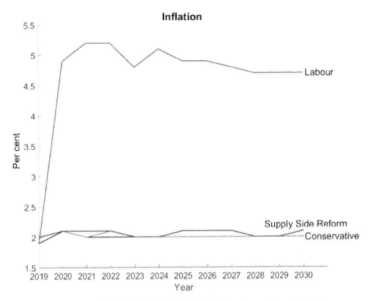

Source: Meenagh and Minford (2020); Minford (2020); other author calculations.

Figure 7.1   Inflation under different projections (%)

CONCLUSIONS – FISCAL POLICY PROGRAMMES AFTER THE ENDING OF THE VIRUS LOCKDOWN

There is a need for fiscal expansion to lift the economy off the ZLB and return power to monetary policy. With Brexit creating a strong post-Brexit supply side, a Conservative government would have an opportunity to spend more, on top of using the growing public finance surplus, and also cut taxes, so stimulating longer-term supply-side growth. Our calculations suggest it could safely pursue this Fiscal Fund Plus strategy and still hit a safe 60% debt/GDP ratio well before 2027. The actual Conservative manifesto is far more cautious than this, with a political decision having been taken to minimize any fiscal risks.

Labour's plans are in a quite different category, since they plan wide nationalization, including lately of telecoms, as well as a four-day week, and a variety of other spending increases, totalling about £80 billion p.a., all these non-capital spending increases to be paid for by higher taxes.

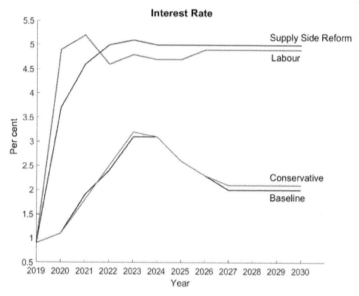

Source: Meenagh and Minford (2020); Minford (2020); other author calculations.

Figure 7.2   Interest rate under different projections (%)

These plans would severely damage the supply side and growth. Their plans are also to borrow an extra £55 billion per year to be added to infrastructure spending. The result of these policies would very likely be a large short-term sterling crisis, causing inflation to spike, and forcing the bank to raise interest rates sharply. While this would rapidly end the ZLB, it would do so in a way that effectively stopped monetary policy from being free to stimulate the economy. The cure would be worse than the disease.

As far as the long term is concerned, these policies would cause a severe weakening of the public sector balance sheet, with the debt/ GDP ratio rising to about 90% and future tax revenues down over 20%, precipitating fears of long-run insolvency. There would be a large fiscal gap, needing to be closed by further tax rises.

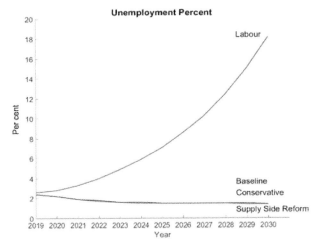

Source: Meenagh and Minford (2020); Minford (2020); other author calculations.

Figure 7.3 *Unemployment under different projections (%)*

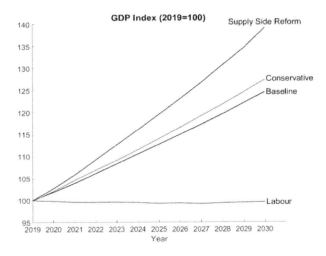

Source: Meenagh and Minford (2020); Minford (2020); other author calculations.

Figure 7.4 *GDP index under different projections (2019 = 100)*

REFERENCES

Hodge Bank (2020), *Quarterly Economic Bulletin*, July, accessed 29 August 2020 at https://hodgebank.co.uk/wp-content/uploads/2020/07/Hodge-QEB-July-2020.pdf.

Meenagh, D. and P. Minford (2020), 'Modelling coronavirus behaviour', in Hodge Bank (2020), *Quarterly Economic Bulletin*, July, accessed 29 August 2020 at https://hodgebank.co.uk/wp-content/uploads/2020/07/Hodge-QEB-July-2020.pdf.

Minford, P. (2020), 'Is recovery beginning?', in Hodge Bank (2020), *Quarterly Economic Bulletin*, July, accessed 29 August 2020 at https://hodgebank.co.uk/wp-content/uploads/2020/07/Hodge-QEB -July-2020.pdf.

Minford, P., with S. Gupta, V.P.M. Le, V. Mahambare and Y. Xu (2015), *Should Britain Leave the EU? An Economic Analysis of a Troubled Relationship*, 2nd edition, Cheltenham, UK and Northampton, MA, USA: Edward Elgar Publishing.

Minford, P. and Y. Xu (2018), 'Classical or gravity: which trade model best matches the UK facts?' *Open Economies Review*, **29** (3), 579–611, accessed 27 August 2020 at http://orca.cf.ac.uk/108158/2/10.1007 %252Fs11079-017-9470-z.pdf.

8. Public spending within the new fiscal programme

As we noted earlier in this book, central planning of the economy suffers from an insuperable information deficit, so that decentralized markets in general are superior. Nevertheless, in most capitalist systems, the government is pressed into service to organize certain economic functions as either a buyer/retailer or a producer. The main areas are defence, healthcare and education, plus, of course, public administration. Much of this was privatized by the Thatcher government in the 1980s. The private sector was appointed supplier of many services the government had hitherto carried out, such as cleaning hospitals and schools, building roads, providing electricity. In the National Health Service (NHS), where politics determined that healthcare should be provided at state expense free at the point of consumption, the private sector was brought in to supply healthcare services as far as possible through the 'NHS internal market', which extended to hospitals (which became private trusts) and GP services (which became private partnerships). Since then, schools have also been provided by private firms under the aegis of 'free schools', where parents can in effect spend an education voucher from the taxpayer on a competing private provider.

In practice, the government has called in private sector firms to organize the provision of government services. Some of these firms – such as Carillion – have collapsed under the strain, illustrating that the executive function of government is a major challenge. The question of how government executive actions should be managed is one that has no clear, definitive answer; instead, one must be found by trial and error. For example, in ancient Rome tax collection was carried out by private agents, 'tax farmers', who then transferred tax proceeds to Rome. We would not think that Her Majesty's Revenue & Customs (HMRC) should become an agency to delegate tax collection to private firms. However, it is a fact that HMRC collaborates actively with a legion of private accountants representing the businesses and people they tax. This collaboration under the tax laws appears to generate the tax revenues the laws mandate, with efficient use of information. In the reforms of taxation discussed in the last chapter, we assumed implicitly that this system would continue in being.

HMRC is also in charge of distributing state benefits, now renamed tax credits. This is another complex function and, arguably, HMRC has the expertise to levy negative as much as positive taxes. The difference, however, lies in the clientele: whereas taxpayers are by construction better off, because they are able to pay taxes, benefit recipients are poor and generally unable to hire accountants to deal with any tax–benefit system complexities. Hence, HMRC must find the resources internally to communicate effectively with this vast impoverished clientele. The rollout of the new universal benefit has accordingly been full of difficulties.

During the coronavirus crisis, the NHS has had to lead government activities not merely to treat the virus but also to organize new supplies of drugs and clinical machinery such as ventilators, while also coordinating research on new drugs, treatments and vaccines. It appears in the process to have made rapid and large-scale changes in its operating methods. While many failures can be pointed to, the fact is that this is a generally effective state firm. Like all firms, it is having to work out the balance between top-down and delegated structures. In terms (Coase, 1937) there are transactions costs in delegation that top-down structures can eliminate, while, on the other hand, delegation can allow more experimentation in the organization.

We live in an age of giant firms, many of them multinational with larger payrolls than governments. There is nothing to tell us a priori how government activities should be executed, only that there must be a market test of overall effectiveness policing any system that emerges. The Thatcher government inherited nationalized industries that failed such market tests: consumers were expropriated by the vested interests gathered in these industries. The long list of privatizations that followed restored consumer power in various ways, including a big rollout of new regulators. Today, we are in a position to re-evaluate how these structures are working, having discovered that it is possible to have government firms active in the marketplace and yet prevent them from rent-seeking at the consumer's expense as the nationalized industries once did.

So, the message of this chapter is a pragmatic one. Government has problems to solve and functions to discharge; and it must find effective means to do so, which could well include a role for government firms or equivalent executive agencies.

Local authorities have found themselves in an idiosyncratic position, both as partial service providers and as buyers of private services. These authorities are the arms of government that get closest to the citizen, providing local services such as rubbish collection, street cleaning and, above all, social care, but also buses, policing and urban road planning. In practice, there are few alternative providers of these services, because their provision is intimately bound up with local democracy; the clients who pay for and receive these services have strong views about them that greatly influence local voting. One can think of them as community management concerns locally organized and supported, with decisions informed by local preferences; they fit into the frameworks for local public goods set out by Elinor Ostrom (Ostrom, 1990), who won the Nobel Prize for her innovative thinking about the costs and benefits of these mechanisms. Their role is to organize the local 'commons' so that the benefits are maximized, with the costs spread fairly around the community.

Take, for example, social care. It is well known that it is cheaper to look after old people in their own homes, often with the cooperation of other family members. To make this possible, the public purse needs to offer help in the home. When home care breaks down, old people end up in hospital, at hugely greater cost to the taxpayer. Yet, time and again, 'social care packages' that enable old people to return home are unavailable. Here we have a role for the local authority to identify the extent of this problem of the commons and to be given a channel for resources from the central taxpayer to fund it. This role is analogous to the role local authorities take in urban road planning; road building is a central government function but efficiently informed by local authority advice.

Under the Thatcher governments, a strategy of 'reinventing government' was formulated. Its motivating inspiration was privatization; but if privatization was impossible, it was argued, then government departments could mimic the private sector by being given precise executive missions, with clear performance targets. Out of this strategy were born 'next steps' agencies of this type, such as the Passport Office and DVLA. HMRC can be viewed as another example, with an executive mission to raise the government's revenues from the taxes decreed by Parliament. This agency model has therefore been widely used and has been generally successful. In many ways it was an easy step to execute, as the Civil Service was already organized along lines that separated off executive functions of government within ministries.

However, the challenge now faced in reforming government involves the central government not so much hiving off functions, whether to the private sector or executive agencies, but rather it requires the central government to collaborate with decentralized local authorities answerable to different (local) electorates in delivering services that complement central government functions such as the NHS. In this process, the central government has an essential enabling and directing role. The new strategy could be called 'reinventing joined-up government' or 'coordinating government' in the delivery of community services vital to social efficiency. This is not just a matter of central funding of local services; it also involves joining information sources distributed through the government machine and tailoring new funding to newly emerging needs in each service branch.

Already, efforts are made by police, social services and the NHS to coordinate information on families with which they all regularly have dealings – 'Troubled Families' (TF) as they are officially known. This TF Programme has been evaluated with mixed results. Efforts to conduct a rigorous analysis of family outcomes are ongoing as the evaluation establishes a robust comparative group outside of the programme. By March 2019, comparative data indicated that the programme had reduced the number of looked-after children, as well as the number of custodial sentences and convictions. However, in areas such as employment, children in need, health, and school attendance, evidence was either mixed, showed little change, or had not yet been possible to analyse. The 2019 cost–benefit analysis suggested that the programme had resulted in economic and fiscal benefits to the taxpayer and wider society. These benefits had mainly been realized through reductions in the number of children in care and youth offending (see Bate, Bellis and Loft, 2020).

So, although it has been reported that social outcomes for these Troubled Families have not much improved as a result, the principle of such coordination needs to be more widely applied in solving local problems, because it brings to bear the mass of locally available information in attempting to solve local problems. Many of these problems should not be as intractable as reducing anti-social behaviour among a hardened group of local citizens; for example, ensuring that social care packages are available to old people who otherwise land up in hospital is a much more achievable administrative objective. It involves information about local problems being reported upwards to the centre, and the centre responding downwards to the local communities with enabling budgets and relevant information from different parts of the government machine.

Personal data must remain private but this does not exclude generic data sharing, as is done routinely in economic research. The objective is to continuously adapt local services to local needs via flexible funding flows. This could be called a National Social Care Service (NSCS), paralleling the NHS. This NSCS has the vital function of partnering with families in delivering social care – an issue rising fast to the top of the political agenda as the number of old people with care needs escalates. Central to this partnership will be a settlement of the 'Who pays?' issue. Currently, families pay all costs until the cared-for person's resources run out entirely, at which point the state pays for whatever care it deems adequate. However, this is a system devoid of state insurance, where private insurance is expensive and often unavailable. Here there is a case for a new National Insurance Contribution (NIC) for social care; this contribution would entitle families to state payment for social care. It was because of the need for such insurance that in the last chapter we advised the retention of National Insurance, even though its insurance element has been steadily debased. For those who prefer private insurance it would be possible to contract out of this new NIC.

One issue that bedevils government agencies is the measurement of efficiency in service delivery. In terms of pure efficiency, measured by the government headcounts and other resources in delivering services in the abstract, it may well be that government today has reached a peak after a decade of austerity that squeezed all spending budgets relentlessly, especially local authority budgets. Treasury folk wisdom has it that only by such squeezing are spending agents inside the government ever forced to find available efficiencies; no one outside these agents' domains knows enough to identify these 'deep inefficiencies' that are difficult and troublesome to remove, and the agents themselves avoid tackling them until the pressure for cuts becomes otherwise intolerable. Only then will they confront these intractable problems in their machines. Much of this may well be true, as the experience of the past ten years has revealed. Who would have thought public services such as the police and local authorities could continue to function after such massive continuing cuts? Table 8.1 shows that total public expenditure fell from 44.7% of gross domestic product (GDP) in 2009–10 to 37.9% of GDP in 2018–19 – an unprecedented fall of nearly 7% of GDP. Yet, the public services have absorbed these cuts by one means or another and continue to survive, carrying out their main functions. In fact, it is their failure to carry out new functions in decentralized service provision that leads to the demand for coordination; there is no generalized failure, rather a spotty failure that points not to a shortage of general resources but to inability to move these resources locally to where they are needed. Fortunately, as we showed in Chapter 5 on fiscal policy, there is large scope for increasing resources being spent by government in the next decade and a half. So, more resources can kickstart the new flexibility and the new government delivery structures in the marketplace.

COMPETITION IN THE PRIVATIZED SECTORS

When privatization was pursued in the 1980s, the aim was to move as fast as possible to full competition, while in the short run, regulation would try to mimic competition. However, this aim has not been achieved. These sectors are still heavily reliant on regulators: we have innumerable offices regulating an endless array of industries – water (OFWAT), railways (OFRAIL), electricity (OFGEM), telecoms (OFCOM) – on and on the OFlist goes. Regulation has almost become the British disease – ironic, considering our aim of reducing EU regulation.

We need to renew that long-term aim of introducing real competition into these industries. Each regulatory agency should be tasked with producing a plan to introduce free entry mechanisms into their industry, enabling the agency either to be abolished or to have its remit limited solely to the ineliminable public good part of the industry. Arguably, in some of these industries, there is a natural monopoly element that is a public good. In water, for example, the rivers that provide the water are a public good, owned collectively; how they are used and their water quality is something the state must control in the public interest. Similarly, electricity is supplied to a National Grid that is publicly provided and shared between electricity companies. Nevertheless, there are ways around the state getting involved. These facilities can be jointly paid for according to negotiated contracts, much as airlines share airport space via contracts for 'slots'. In the case of railway track, a frequent model is that operating companies take ownership of track where they are the most frequent user but must agree contracts for rights of use with other operators. This is analogous to internet platforms with services to sell allowing access for competitors. There can be regulative laws enforcing such access without having to have a regulator.

Table 8.1   *Public expenditure aggregates, 1976–77 to 2019–20[a]*

	Public sector current expenditure			Depre-ciation	Public sector net investment			Total managed expenditure		
	Nom-inal £ billion	Real terms £ billion	Per cent of GDP	Nom-inal £ billion	Nom-inal £ billion	Real terms £ billion	Per cent of GDP	Nom-inal £ billion	Real terms £ billion	Per cent of GDP
1976–77	51.2	298.0	36.1	6.4	6.4	37.4	4.5	64.1	372.9	45.1
1977–78	57.5	294.2	34.7	7.4	5.2	26.8	3.2	70.2	358.8	42.3
1978–79	66.1	304.0	34.4	8.4	5.2	23.9	2.7	79.7	366.5	41.5
1979–80	79.6	313.2	34.2	10.0	5.8	22.7	2.5	95.3	375.1	41.0
1980–81	96.8	319.8	36.2	12.1	5.8	19.2	2.2	114.7	378.8	42.9
1981–82	110.8	331.1	37.2	13.2	4.1	12.4	1.4	128.2	382.9	43.0
1982–83	121.6	338.8	37.2	13.9	6.1	17.1	1.9	141.6	394.4	43.3
1983–84	131.3	349.0	36.7	14.6	7.6	20.2	2.1	153.4	407.8	42.9
1984–85	142.0	357.3	36.8	14.8	7.3	18.4	1.9	164.1	412.8	42.5
1985–86	150.5	359.1	35.6	14.4	6.3	15.1	1.5	171.3	408.6	40.4
1986–87	158.7	363.5	34.9	14.9	4.8	11.0	1.1	178.4	408.7	39.2
1987–88	169.6	368.0	33.2	14.9	4.7	10.2	0.9	189.3	410.6	37.1
1988–89	176.3	359.2	31.0	15.8	3.8	7.7	0.7	195.9	399.1	34.4
1989–90	191.1	361.4	30.5	16.8	9.0	17.0	1.4	216.8	410.1	34.6
1990–91	208.1	363.8	30.7	16.7	10.3	17.9	1.5	235.1	411.0	34.7
1991–92	232.0	383.6	32.5	15.4	13.5	22.3	1.9	260.9	431.4	36.6
1992–93	252.1	406.6	34.3	15.3	14.0	22.7	1.9	281.5	453.9	38.3
1993–94	266.2	419.0	34.2	15.6	11.9	18.8	1.5	293.7	462.4	37.7
1994–95	277.6	431.8	34.0	15.7	12.3	19.1	1.5	305.5	475.2	37.4
1995–96	291.2	439.4	33.9	15.7	12.6	19.0	1.5	319.4	482.0	37.1
1996–97	300.3	437.8	32.8	16.0	7.6	11.1	0.8	323.9	472.2	35.3
1997–98	308.2	446.4	32.1	18.7	6.5	9.3	0.7	333.4	482.8	34.8
1998–99	316.6	452.6	31.6	18.8	7.8	11.1	0.8	343.1	490.6	34.2
1999–00	327.5	466.4	31.3	19.4	9.2	13.1	0.9	356.1	507.2	34.1
2000–01	349.1	486.3	31.8	20.0	9.2	12.8	0.8	378.3	526.9	34.4
2001–02	366.9	506.1	32.1	20.9	16.4	22.6	1.4	404.2	557.5	35.4
2002–03	394.2	530.5	32.8	22.8	20.8	27.9	1.7	437.8	589.2	36.5
2003–04	430.8	568.0	34.0	22.9	23.8	31.4	1.9	477.5	629.6	37.6
2004–05	463.5	595.1	34.9	24.5	28.9	37.0	2.2	516.9	663.6	38.9
2005–06	490.8	614.0	34.7	25.9	29.7	37.2	2.1	546.4	683.5	38.7

	Public sector current expenditure			Depreciation	Public sector net investment			Total managed expenditure		
	Nominal £ billion	Real terms £ billion	Per cent of GDP	Nominal £ billion	Nominal £ billion	Real terms £ billion	Per cent of GDP	Nominal £ billion	Real terms £ billion	Per cent of GDP
2006–07	513.7	624.1	34.5	27.2	31.0	37.6	2.1	571.9	694.8	38.4
2007–08	544.4	645.4	34.9	28.2	33.9	40.2	2.2	606.5	719.1	38.9
2008–09	577.1	666.1	36.9	31.1	53.5	61.7	3.4	661.7	763.8	42.3
2009–10	610.0	694.3	39.4	32.5	52.7	60.0	3.4	695.2	791.2	44.9
2010–11	637.7	712.5	39.7	33.9	45.7	51.1	2.8	717.4	801.5	44.7
2011–12	645.9	712.3	39.1	35.4	35.9	39.6	2.2	717.3	791.0	43.5
2012–13	655.9	709.1	38.3	36.6	39.3	42.5	2.3	731.8	791.1	42.8
2013–14	665.2	706.1	37.3	38.0	30.7	32.6	1.7	733.8	779.0	41.2
2014–15	674.8	707.3	36.4	39.0	36.6	38.4	2.0	750.4	786.5	40.5
2015–16	682.6	709.8	35.7	40.1	34.1	35.4	1.8	756.8	786.9	39.6
2016–17	692.7	704.5	34.8	40.8	38.5	39.1	1.9	772.0	785.2	38.8
2017–18	707.8	707.8	34.4	41.0	40.7	40.7	2.0	789.5	789.5	38.4
2018–19	733.0	722.1	34.6	40.9	39.0	38.4	1.8	812.9	800.7	38.4
2019–20	745.3	722.8	34.2	42.2	46.6	45.2	2.1	834.0	808.8	38.3

Notes:
a. Outturn data in this table up to 2017–18 fall within the scope of National Statistics.
b. Real terms figures are the nominal figures adjusted to 2017–18 price levels using GDP deflators from the Office for National Statistics (released 29 June 2018).
c. This excludes the temporary effects of banks being classified to the public sector.
Source: HM Treasury Public Expenditure Statistical Analyses (PESA).

INFRASTRUCTURE

The biggest area of government spending is on infrastructure. Here there has been confusion, as incoming governments bring with them their pet projects of national renewal. The most recent example was the Cameron/ Osborne project for HS2, which has been dogged by controversy. The attempt to justify it by cost–benefit criteria was never convincing, with absurdly high valuations of time saved in travel. In the end it has been given the go-ahead by the Johnson government on the different and reasonable grounds of need for extra North–South rail capacity, which to provide by expanding existing routes would have proved highly dis- ruptive. There is now a UK National Infrastructure Commission, akin to the Office for Budget Responsibility, with a brief to review infrastructure projects according to proper criteria – this is a welcome development. As the Johnson government gears up to spend an extra £20 billion a year on infrastructure, it should follow the advice of this new advisory agency on how to spend it.

EVALUATING PUBLIC SPENDING PROPOSALS

What the HS2 project reveals is that it was never seriously evaluated from an economic viewpoint; it was pushed forward for purely political reasons. This process is bound to cause waste. Instead, we should look at what projects achieve in lowering the private sector's costs, that is, raising its productivity, a supply-side approach focused on effects on the economy's productivity. This would put it on a par with the way we evaluate tax changes (see above): when taxes are cut they lower private sector costs and so raise GDP. This analysis can and should be extended to public current spending, such as on health and education. Though 'current', they are every bit as important to productivity as infrastructure, which is 'capital'.

Endless controversy has surrounded the issue of how much private firms should be involved in delivering health and education spending. Yet again, this should be resolved by analysing the effect on costs and productivity. On the whole, private firms operating under competitive supply conditions are more efficient than public monopolies. However, there is also the key question of transaction costs, emphasized by Ronald Coase (Coase, 1937); sometimes there is simply too much complexity in splitting up provision inside a large organization. The balance has to be discovered, probably by trial and error. For example, with schools, private provision of 'free schools' has been successful to some degree in improving education (Lehain, 2018; Perera, 2019) with few problems of interaction with local authority provision; the schools involved can deal effectively with parents, with little need to coordinate with each other. By contrast, arm's length transactions by hived-off GP surgery businesses and hospital trusts may have created bureaucratic costs within the NHS that exceed the gains from private sector competition (e.g., Dehn, 2007; Pollock, 2007).

THE 'PRODUCTIVITY PUZZLE'

One area of the economy where demands are made for government action – for example, in the provision of more training of unskilled workers – is the low growth of measured productivity, especially since the financial crisis struck in 2008. UK productivity growth slowed by more than in most other countries.

However, before we rush into action with government interventions in training and education, we need to be sure of the facts. We know that the consumer price index (CPI) measure is vulnerable to quality change, the introduction of new products, and the provision of free goods/services. These features are particularly prominent in ICT-intensive industries that are especially important in the UK's service-dominated economy. If the CPI is overstated, it undermines the measures of both productivity and real wages used in this work. It is certainly odd to see widespread pessimism over productivity trends coexisting with equally widespread concerns over the job-destroying effects of ICT trends. Efforts are being made in recent research to improve price measures for the factors identified above (e.g., Aghion et al., 2018). But, so far, little progress seems to have been made by official statistical agencies.

Aghion et al. point out that what these agencies do is impute to the new products the same inflation as the old products, then assign them their sales share weight in the total. However, plainly, this disregards the price fall when the new product enters disruptively; think of Amazon shifting us from daily shopping travel to home delivery; or Google saving us the trip to the public library; or telecommuting in place of distant meetings; or paying fines/taxes online instead of at some tax office.

Aghion et al. substitute the price change from the old product to the new product. The result is startling: in France, rather close to the UK in shopping patterns, the inflation rate has been overstated by 0.7% p.a. in recent years, and an average of 0.4% p.a. in the earlier years (vs 0.6% in the US throughout). Notice the increase over the recent past, offsetting a fair proportion of the official slowdown in productivity and real wage growth.

It seems reasonable to treat the estimated overstatement of the CPI in France as at least a preliminary guide for the UK whose shopping patterns are reasonably similar, and whose economy is similarly dominated by services. If one applies these French corrections to UK real wage and productivity data, it turns out there is little difference in either real wages or productivity per hour between the recent past and the previous period. Table 8.2 shows official GDP/hour for the UK. It can be seen that if 0.4% is added to the 1979–2007 figure, and 0.7% to the 2008–now figure, we obtain 0.96% p.a. recently, against 1.1% p.a. before.

If we do the same for real wages (Table 8.3), the situation is similar. The later period real wage growth becomes 0.8% p.a., while the earlier period becomes 1.01% p.a.

Table 8.2   *Official GDP/hour for the UK*

Period	Real GDP/Labour Hour Growth Rate
1955–78	0.90%
1979–2007	0.71%: adjusted 1.1%
2008–now	0.26%: adjusted 0.96%

Source: Office for National Statistics.

Table 8.3   *Real wage growth*

Period	Wage/CPI Growth Rate
1955–78	0.56%
1979–2007	0.61%: adjusted 1.01%
2008–now	0.10%: adjusted 0.8%

Source: Office for National Statistics, as adjusted for CPI correction.

Another way of getting some perspective on the effect of disruption on the price index is to take the share of transport and communications in the CPI, which is 17.4%, and imagine that due to the rise in digital connectivity roughly half its cost has been saved in the past decade; this approximately matches a drop over the period in car traffic per capita of about 8%. That would give an overstatement of the CPI of about 0.8% a year, similar to Aghion et al.'s estimate for France.

However, it is most likely that productivity will be greatly affected by the coronavirus crisis, with many changes going on in industrial structure. Our main concern will be to ensure the labour market returns to full employment. Because it is so flexible and workers move easily across sectors, this is likely. Increasing use of artificial intelligence and automation will make the earlier productivity figures look like ancient history.

POLICY FOR THE NORTHERN REVIVAL

A major challenge is to bring the North's income up to the level of that of London and the South. As many people have pointed out, a good start would be to improve the infrastructure of the North, which has lagged behind the South's, especially in transport. HS2 has become controversial because of cost overruns, but the main argument for it is not faster journeys, which is where the cost–benefit has focused, but simply that it is the most economical way to produce the extra North–South journey and freight capacity needed because of increased congestion on road and rail. Doing this by expanding the current rail capacity would be expensively disruptive. HS3 should go ahead fast as well, together with the improvements promised in the Northern Powerhouse programme.

The usual assumption when the problems of the North are mentioned relative to the South is that 'more should be spent' on Northern infrastructure. This may be true but it misses the point. The essential point is that the North needs to achieve stronger cost competitiveness. The South achieves its results because it is highly competitive in world markets. This is certainly partly due to good infrastructure. But mainly it is the result of creating products and services that are in high demand internationally. In our Liverpool Model of the UK as a whole, the level of GDP is governed by UK cost competitiveness. This in turn is the result of the level of tax net of its opposites, regulatory costs on business.

In a parallel piece of work analysing how UK growth occurred during the Thatcher years, Minford and Meenagh (2020) showed that it was related to the cutting back of tax rates and regulation during the 1980s. This led to a surge in entrepreneurship, which boosted productivity growth. Essentially, the same ideas apply to the North as apply to the UK as a whole. The North, after all, is simply one part of the same UK organism.

It is helpful to start by understanding how London itself became such a competitive economy. Plainly, much money has been spent on its transport infrastructure. But much of this has been in response to the economic activity it has created, that is, to its success from other causes. Essentially, this success has been tied up with the development of the City of London, the world's top financial centre. This in turn came from the provision and development of huge amounts of land in the docklands, feeding a demand for the City's services across the world. This City industry in turn was fed by supplies of skilled labour, plentiful in the UK due to expanding higher education and a liberal approach to skilled immigration. Other supply-side factors were the common law courts that made the UK an attractive place for dispute resolution, and that ample supply of land that gave the City space to expand.

The trade models we have looked at in earlier chapters give us corroborating insights. After abandoning EU protection of food and manufacturing, it will be the City and other service industries that expand as costs, especially of land, inflated by protection, come down.

Looking towards the North, what are the policy implications? Northern cities now have increased powers vested in mayors, just as London has had. This gives them an opportunity to think and act strategically to reduce costs and increase their regional competitiveness. If these cities and their cooperating surrounding regions can identify the infrastructure they need to support these moves, they now have a government strongly willing to oblige by providing it through central government funding. However, to be fair to central government, this is not entirely new. Money has flowed from the centre to well-organized Northern initiatives for some time. One only has to look at roads around Manchester or expenditures on the old docklands of central Liverpool to be aware that central government has spent liberally on Northern development where needs have been identified. Essentially, the system for providing infrastructure is demand led by local needs, these in turn being created by economic growth.

The failures of the North to grow as fast as London cannot therefore be laid at the feet of central government unwillingness to spend on northern infrastructure. It looks rather as if it is the failure of the North to grow that has slowed down the associated infrastructure provision.

It might then well be asked: how can central government policy break into this slow-growth Northern equilibrium? The answer is to be found in the way the Thatcher government broke into the low-growth UK equilibrium – by lowering taxes and similar regulative restraints on cost competitiveness. Lower taxes work across the whole economy. By lowering general taxes and easing economy-wide regulations, economic activity is boosted across the whole economy. But such moves today, with a congested Southern economy, will primarily benefit the North, because that is where there is spare capacity. One can think of the process as a two-stage one. Cutting taxes and regulative costs will boost competitiveness across the UK, but because of Southern congestion, Southern costs will rise in response, while Northern costs will not. Hence, the net effect will be to lower Northern costs and raise Northern competitiveness, while leaving Southern largely unchanged.

It follows that, in general, the way to boost the North is to cut taxes and regulative costs across the UK as a whole, and then respond in the usual way to the resulting infrastructure demands from the North. It is not to artificially boost spending on Northern infrastructure independently of demand-led needs. The exception would be if some particular infrastructure project would itself stimulate some identifiable development;

Table 8.4   *Long run effects of different tax/regulative measures on North and South – each package costed at £10 billion*

	% GDP North	% GDP South
Cut standard rate of income tax	1.1	0.5
Cut Corporation tax rate	0.8	0.4
Cut marginal tax rate and regulative burden on Entrepreneurs/ SMEs	12	21
Increase infrastructure spending in North	1.6	-

Source: Author calculations, based on Gai, Meenagh and Minford (2020).

however, this has to be carefully evaluated. Too often, infrastructure created to 'spur development' creates roads or bridges that 'lead to nowhere', that is, to areas with little going on. In principle, infrastructure spending lowers costs for business by raising productivity. For example, one only has to think back to the way railways promoted development in the US. But, of course, the railway era in which this promotion occurred also came to an end once railways went to most places. In the North today transport infrastructure already covers the area. To contribute, new transport links must improve on existing ones by lowering costs.

We have embodied these ideas in a Regional UK Model, which is derived from the same supply-side approach as originally taken in the Liverpool Model, used to advise Margaret Thatcher's governments. In this model, each region, North and South, has a labour market that distributes employment into general goods/services production and also into house building. Labour supply depends on net of tax wages, adjusted for prices including house prices. The cost competitiveness of general industries determines their success at home relative to imports and in foreign markets; apart from productivity, whose growth is affected by taxes and regulations on entrepreneurs, cost competitiveness depends on wages. A general tax cut – for example, of VAT or income tax – encourages labour supply and so lowers wages, raising cost competitiveness; net exports rise and the economy expands. The percentage effect on GDP expansion is higher in the North than in the South because in the North labour is more plentiful, and therefore rises more as net of tax wages rises.

We have fitted this model to the UK data (Table 8.4), finding the coefficients that get closest to matching the UK facts. From a policy viewpoint, what interests us is the GDP effect of different tax cuts costing the Treasury the same, set for illustration at £10 billion each. What we see here is that all these measures, except the top rate cuts, have a bigger positive impact on the North than on the South. The main message of these changes is that a 'cocktail' of tax cuts and regulative easing if all were combined would generate a powerful stimulus to growth, especially in the North. The top two tax cuts improve labour market competitiveness and work by increasing market share vs foreign competition. The cut in the marginal tax rate and the regulative burden on entrepreneurs, together with better infrastructure, raise the rate of innovation and productivity growth; they boost the entrepreneurial economy, a vital element in the new industrial structure post-COVID and post-Brexit.

REFERENCES

Aghion, P., A. Bergeaud, T. Boppart and S. Bunel (2018), 'Firm dynamics and growth measurement in France', *Journal of the European Economic Association*, **16** (4), 933–56.

Bate, A., A. Bellis and P. Loft (2020), *Briefing Paper Number 07585, 22 January 2020: The Troubled Families Programme (England)*, House of Commons Library, accessed 31 August 2020 at https://researchbriefings.files.parliament.uk/documents/CBP-7585/CBP-7585.pdf.

Coase, R. (1937), 'The nature of the firm', *Economica*, 4, 386–405.

Dehn, T. (2007), 'Private provision in the UK National Health Service', *Annals of the Royal College of Surgeons of England*, **89** (4), 337.

Gai, Y., D. Meenagh and P. Minford (2020), 'A regional model of the UK North and South', unpublished Economics Working Paper, Cardiff Business School.

Lehain, M. (2018), 'The results are in: free schools are working', *CAPX*, accessed 31 August 2020 at https://capx.co/the-results-are-in-free-schools-are-working.

Minford, L. and D. Meenagh (2020), 'Supply-side policy and economic growth: a case study of the UK', *Open Economies Review*, **31** (1), 159–93.

Ostrom, E. (1990), *Governing the Commons: The Evolution of Institutions for Collective Action*, Cambridge, UK: Cambridge University Press.

Perera, N. (2019), 'Has the free schools programme been a success?', *Prospect*, 17 October, accessed 31 August 2020 at https://www.prospectmagazine.co.uk/politics/has-the-free-schools-programme-been-success-education-gove-williamson.

Pollock, A. (2007), 'The case against private provision in the NHS', *Annals of the Royal College of Surgeons of England*, **89** (4), 338–9.

9. Conclusions

There are many aspects of UK economic policy that require overhauling for the British economy to function well and satisfy the aspirations of the British people to have strong growth within a fully employed economy. Leaving the EU, whose economic policies have held the economy back over the past 40 years, gives our government an opportunity to reform not just those EU policies, in trade, regulation and migration, but also the many other areas where matters have been allowed to drift on in an unsatisfactory way. Often, the excuse for that drift was that EU membership might in practice prevent change, since other EU countries might raise objections of various sorts, based on uniformity and a 'level playing field'. It is certainly true that EU directives intruded further and further into UK practice over the past 40 years.

Hence, in this book I have examined the way all the critical levers of UK policy are now being used and how they could be reformed to create a 'new dawn' for the UK economy. In the first part I examined the detailed 'micro' effects of trade tariffs and other barriers, taxation and regulation, and I have proposed that we embark on a radical free trade policy towards the rest of the world, while opening up the economy to innovation and industrial change by a pro-competitive regulative agenda, led by market needs, replacing the EU's social interventionism. I have also sketched out a new tax system, with a wide consumption base and the lowest possible marginal tax rates, to help spur the entrepreneurial innovation required.

I went on in the second part to review the workings of fiscal and monetary policy, and how these powerful levers that control aggregate demand could be used to support this reform agenda. Before the COVID crisis, the dominant pro-EU establishment constantly argued that fiscal deficits must be kept down to ensure solvency. However, in practice, this agenda simply prevented radical reform; this excuse was even used, in conjunction with fallacious projections of economic ruin from Brexit, to argue that we 'could not afford' to leave the EU. However, the UK is a sovereign borrower that has never defaulted on its public debts and, therefore, its solvency has rarely been in question. It has taken the

COVID crisis to reveal that it can run immense deficits while remaining solvent: it now seems likely the COVID debt will reach £350 billion. Yet, when issued in today's markets at interest rates of 0.4% and less on very long-term maturities, its cost to future taxpayers will be nugatory; over the coming year, the Bank of England needs to offload the public debt it holds into the markets at current low rates to ensure money is controlled, and with it inflation, while keeping the average interest rate on existing public debt as low as possible. What this book does is to quantify the long-term limits placed on fiscal policy by solvency; I have projected long-term balance sheet outcomes of different policies, including the outcome from the COVID crisis. It turns out that what matters in the long term is growth, as this provides the revenue base for public spending, so ensuring solvency. Fiscal deficits for a period can enable reform that stimulates growth. I have set out how taxes can be cut and vital spending undertaken that will generate this growth, on top of the growth created by the Brexit reforms to tariffs and regulation that cost no revenue. I have also set out how these policies will create 'levelling up' through growth being particularly responsive to these measures in the North; we do not need levelling down of the South, nor do we need a splurge of ill-directed spending in the North. On the contrary, a well-based supply-side agenda will deliver strong growth led by the North, where there is an enormous scope for industrial renaissance.

Brexit and the COVID crisis, coming so soon on the heels of the financial crisis, have put the spotlight on what is wrong with our current economic policies. In this book I have argued that we can put those wrongs right; people are ready for change, having seen the failures of the current dispensation and forcibly expressed their dissatisfaction with the economy's current workings. As we emerge into the recovery from the COVID recession into the post-Brexit world we have an unparalleled opportunity to reform the economic environment into one that creates growth and innovation. This is an opportunity we simply must take.

Index